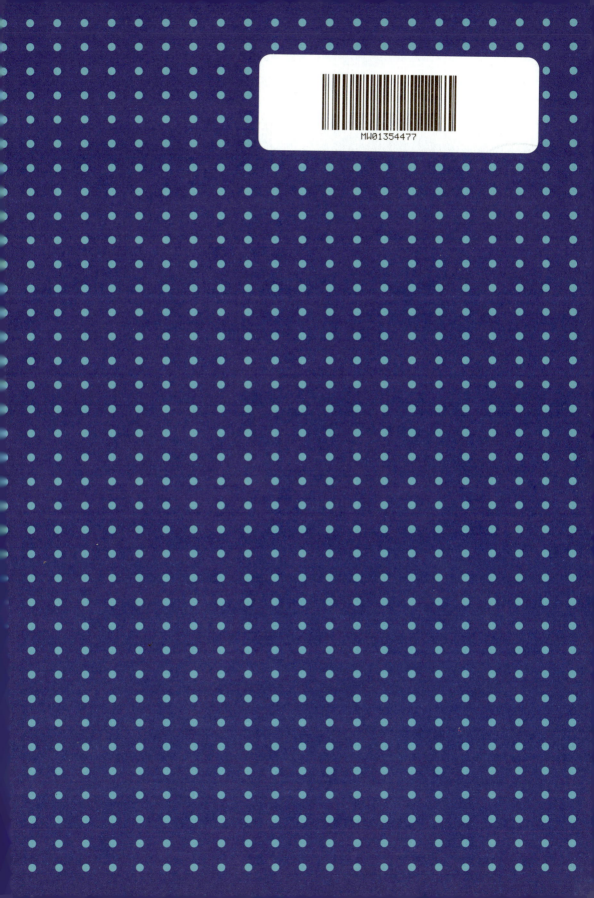

People Powered Money is the result of a project running from 2012-2015, Community Currencies in Action (CCIA). Part-funded by the European Union's Interreg project, CCIA is a transnational project in the community currency field, bringing together expert partners from across north-west Europe and co-ordinating six pilot currencies in the United Kingdom, Belgium, the Netherlands and France.

Drawing on the learnings of these pilots and the broader currency innovation movement, this book provides policymakers and practitioners alike with the information and advice to successfully implement a currency project in their communities. With the right knowledge and support, these can bring significant economic, social and environmental benefits to their users.

Often confined to the margins, community currencies have the potential to become a normal part of economic life. CCIA hopes this book will enable a new generation of community currencies and support their emergence into the mainstream.

PEOPLE POWERED MONEY

PEOPLE POWERED MONEY

Designing, developing & delivering community currencies

People Powered Money
Designing, developing and delivering community currencies

First edition published in paperback in Great Britain in 2015 by

New Economics Foundation
10 Salamanca Place
London SE1 7HB
(0)20 7820 6300
info@neweconomics.org
www.neweconomics.org

creative commons

This book is Licensed under a Creative Commons Attribution-NonCommercial-ShareAlike 3.0 Unported License. Every effort has been made to trace or contact all copyright holders. The publishers will be pleased to make good any omissions or rectify any mistakes brought to their attention at the earliest opportunity. No responsibility can be accepted by the publisher for action taken as a result of information contained in this publication.

A CIP catalogue record for this book is available from the British Library.

Print ISBN: 978-1-908506-78-8 | ePub ISBN: 978-1-908506-80-1

registered charity number 1055254
© April 2015 New Economics Foundation

NEF supports The Forest Stewardship Council [FSC], the leading international forest certification organisation.
All NEF publications are printed on FSC-certified paper.

Project Managed by EDDEPRO Services
Cover illustration Alex Lucas
Design and layout A-Side Studio
Copy edited by Alexis Taylor

Printed and bound in Great Britain by Blackmore, Shaftesbury SP7 8PX

Acknowledgements

This book would not have been possible without the commitment and contributions of our CCIA partners and many external experts who have worked on the topic for many years, as well as, of course, the funding contributed by the European Union's Interreg 4b NorthWest Europe programme.

We would like to acknowledge, first and foremost, those who helped to write *People Powered Money*, especially Leander Bindewald, Alice Martin, Duncan McCann, Tony Greenham and Duncan Thomas.

This book also draws on recent community currency guidebooks in Dutch and French by our colleagues in Belgium and the Netherlands:

Guide pratique de monnaies complémentaires (2013), written by Antoine Attout, Léone Clerc, Amandine Cloot, Antoine Fain, Lise Disneur, Arnaud Marchand and Laurence Roland and published by the Réseau Financement Alternatif in Brussels with the support of the Wallonian government.

Maak je buurt uitmuntend! (2014), written by Bernard Lietaer, Anne Snick and Edgar Kampers, published by the Flemish government.

This book also builds on the CCIA *Community Currency Implementation Framework*, which pooled the experience and knowledge of our partners and of those on whose shoulders we stand. For this we are especially indebted to the work of Henk van Arkel of the Social Trade Organisation (NL), John Rogers (UK/DE), Arthur Brock of the Metacurrency Project (USA), Ludwig Schuster and the late Margrit Kennedy of the Money Network Alliance (DE), to mention just a few.

We are also very grateful to Nigel Dodd and Molly Scott Cato for contributing forewords. Endorsements from such well-known and respected figures demonstrate how far the community currency movement has come in gaining recognition and establishing its credibility within the economics discipline and field of public policy.

Last but not least, we would like to thank Philipp Degens, Jens Martignoni, Ken Barlow, Susan Steed, Julia Slay, Lucie Stephens, Carlos De Freitas and Brett Scott, who have given priceless feedback and support to ensure that the book is not only comprehensive regarding its subject matter, but written and presented in an accessible and stimulating manner.

CONTENTS

16   CCIA Partners
18   Forewords
20   Introduction
22   What is in the book?
24   Key

Part One: How can money better meet our aims?

Chapter 01

30   **REBIRTH OF AN OLD TECHNOLOGY**

34   The historic legacy
35   Modern grassroots origins
38   The new millennials
39   Today's cross-sector fusion

Chapter 02

42   **WHY – COMMUNITY CURRENCIES: MONEY WITH A PURPOSE**

44   Democratising services and organisations
49   Supporting the SME economy
58   Countering inequality and social exclusion
63   Addressing environmental impacts

Chapter 03

68   **WHO – CURRENCIES FOR THE PEOPLE, BY THE PEOPLE**

70   Stakeholders in a currency system
71   Levels of engagement
79   Challenges of a multi-stakeholder project
81   Co-producing a currency

Part Two: Innovating money – a how to

Chapter 04

88 THE PROCESS OF DESIGNING A CURRENCY

90   Non-linear
92   Phase A: Planning
93   Phase B: Building – Piloting
94   Phase C: Continuity options

Chapter 05

98 WHAT – CHOOSING THE KEY FEATURES OF A COMMUNITY CURRENCY

99   Function
101   Denomination & transaction medium
104   Issuance
108   Backing
109   Design specifics
113   Security
114   Market

Chapter 06

116 HOW – IMPLEMENTING AND OPERATING A CURRENCY

118   Organisational structure and governance
120   Finance
126   Legal & compliance
130   ICT

Chapter 07

136 THE IMPORTANCE OF GOOD COMMUNICATIONS

137 Target audiences
138 Key messages
141 Get the message out
146 Maintaining a network

Chapter 08

148 EVALUATION – DEFINING AND MEASURING IMPACT

150 Getting started
151 What to measure
151 When to measure
152 Who to involve
153 How to measure

Chapter 09

158 CONCLUSION – MORE CURRENCIES ARE BETTER THAN ONE

160 End notes
162 Further reading & resources
170 Glossary
180 Index

CCIA partners

Amsterdam East Municipality: a local authority serving 112,000 residents of a long-deprived area of Amsterdam. Committed to investing in social, urban and economic issues, Amsterdam East supports the Makkie, a CCIA pilot currency seeking to build community engagement and empower citizens to create the change they want for their community.

Crédit Municipal de Nantes: a publicly owned enterprise with an economic and social mission, offering credit and mutual savings schemes to residents of the city of Nantes. Crédit Municipal de Nantes plays a strategic role in improving the quality of life of the community it serves and manages the SoNantes, a CCIA-supported currency.

Lambeth

Lambeth Council: a local authority in South London, UK. In collaboration with CCIA and the Brixton Pound, Lambeth Council is working to integrate the community currency into council services and promote its wide usage. This collaboration is an integral part of Lambeth's aim to become Britain's first Co-operative Council — meaning that it will work with local people to design, manage, and deliver services together.

limburg.net

Limburg.net: an inter-municipal, publicly owned waste-disposal company responsible for waste prevention and collection in the province of Limburg and the city of Diest. Together with CCIA, Limburg.net expanded their community currency, the e-Portemonnee, to encourage environmentally sustainable practices by individuals and businesses across the whole region.

New Economics Foundation (NEF): a UK think-tank promoting social, economic and environmental justice. NEF is the UK's leading not-for-profit research institute in the study of money, credit and complementary currencies. Within CCIA, NEF have led on evaluation and communications methods, research into legal and compliance issues, and the production of the collaborative online tool: community-currency.info.

Qoin: a Dutch social enterprise, specialising in the design and implementation of community currencies. As part of CCIA, Qoin have developed a flexible and functional software platform, Qoinware, that is currently used by several community currencies, including the SoNantes and the Brixton Pound. They also launched their own co-operatively owned business-to-business CCIA pilot currency: TradeQoin.

Spice: a social enterprise originating in Wales but now working across the UK, Spice develops agency time-credit systems for communities and public- and voluntary-sector agencies. Having already proven highly successful in addressing inequalities, building stronger communities and empowering citizens, Spice's programmes are being scaled up in partnership with CCIA.

Wales Council for Voluntary Action (WCVA): the voice of the voluntary sector in Wales, representing and campaigning for voluntary organisations, individuals and communities. WCVA is lead partner for CCIA and has monitored the operations of the partnership, as well as co-ordinating member organisations.

Forewords

Just as fish do not see the water that they swim in, so we exist every day in a world where money is shaping and controlling our lives and yet we take it entirely for granted. We do not ask who created that money; or why some people come by it so easily whereas others are always running to catch up. That is a shame, because the design and issue of money is one of the keys to understanding economic injustice, and emancipating ourselves from the debt-based money system is an essential step towards creating a just and sustainable world.

This is why I am delighted by the publication of *People Powered Money*, a book by some of the leading experts in the field of community currency design and implementation. With support from the European Union, Community Currencies in Action (CCIA) is the biggest transnational coalition working towards building a stronger theoretical and practice base for the development of local currency initiatives.

This book draws on the experience of these key pilot projects in community currencies and the broader currency innovation movement, providing policymakers and practitioners with the information and advice they need to successfully implement a currency project in their communities. The idea of a community currency is no longer a marginal one and the time is right for these initiatives to move into the mainstream.

As I know from experience, creating a locally bound currency gives you an unparalleled insight into the way your local economy works and the way money shapes economic power. I am proud to have one of the most successful local currencies – the Bristol Pound – in my political patch. This book will help to share the understanding of that and the other currencies that are liberating many from economic oppression and helping them build vibrant and resilient economies.

Molly Scott Cato Member of the European Parliament for South West England and former Professor of Economics at Roehampton University.

This is an important and timely book. For some years now, we have been witnessing something of a monetary revolution, which consists of an explosion of new forms of money. These vary considerably, and include digital currency technologies such as Bitcoin, new modes of social lending such as Zopa, innovative mobile payment systems such as the M-Pesa, and community currencies such as the SoNantes in France, the Makkie in the Netherlands and the Brixton Pound in the UK.

Alongside this growth in monetary innovation, there has been a surge of interest in the nature of money itself, as people from all walks of life wake up to the fact that the era when there was just one dominant form of money – state fiat money – is over, while others are still catching up on how the old system actually worked. In many ways this is a return to the past: multiple monies were a fact of life until the late 19th century, and have remained so outside the global north, although in terms of scale, diversity and technology, what we are seeing now is also quite new.

The authors argue that there has never before been a movement of this scale and significance in studying and innovating monetary designs from the bottom up. But as exciting and intriguing as these developments are, they also pose urgent questions: how best to understand the nature of money in an era of monetary pluralism; how to evaluate the efficacy of new monetary forms; what kind of regulation (if any) might be called for by their emergence; and what their implications will be for our everyday lives.

Bringing together experts from six European countries, Community Currencies in Action (CCIA) has undertaken invaluable research into one major form of monetary innovation, namely, community currencies. The findings of this collaborative project are presented in this book, drawing important lessons from schemes that are already underway and offering useful advice to people who might be considering launching new initiatives in their own communities.

Besides offering practical advice, the central message of this book is that money really can make a positive difference to our lives and genuinely can enrich the communities in which we live and work. Money is a tool: it's time we used it to our advantage.

Nigel Dodd, Professor in Sociology, London School of Economics and author of *The Social Life of Money* (Princeton University Press, 2014)

Introduction

Money holds many mysteries. Where does it come from? How did it evolve? Who creates it and controls it? Why do we never seem to have enough?

This book will help to unravel some of the mysteries of money and to explain how communities can create their own money.

This might seem outlandish to those with no experience of the community currency movement, but the depth of historical experience and breadth of present-day practice testify to the power and potential of currency innovations to make the world a better place.

The abundance of concepts and terminology that has emerged from the world of currency design can be intimidating for those new to the subject. One way of cutting through this is to think of money – in the broadest sense of the word – as a social technology.

As with any technology, money is designed and implemented to achieve certain objectives. With mainstream money, such as the national or transnational currencies we use every day, these objectives are obscured – precisely because, paradoxically, the medium and usage is so familiar and unremarkable.

However, rather than merely the oil that eases transactions, money – as social technology – can never be 'neutral'. Indeed, this conception has been increasingly challenged by critical economists, who identify negative economic, environmental and societal consequences from how conventional monetary systems are designed and managed.

From their earliest incarnations to most contemporary systems, currencies can be thought of as records of transactions. Whereas previously these records were stored on tablets and then books, today most are kept electronically, in a purely digital form. In fact, new communication technologies are widely predicted to herald the 'end of cash'. In place of handing over a piece of paper or a coin as a record of exchange, computers can now tally transactions much more efficiently.

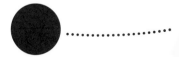

As distant as an entirely paperless economy might still seem in many parts of the world, it will become increasingly widespread due to the advancing digital revolution. Indeed, many aspects of money today already seem in a state of transformation not dissimilar to the overhaul of transportation and production when steam power sparked the industrial revolution. These profound changes bring both great risks and exciting opportunities to reconsider and redesign money to better serve human society and our natural environment.

Community currencies respond to such opportunities and, in contrast to conventional money systems, make their aims explicit. They are technologies designed to help certain communities work together towards desired and commonly understood aims. Far from merely alternative media that leave the wider system of economic exchange and social relations untouched, community currencies are first and foremost instruments of change and empowerment.

What is in the book?

The book is divided into two parts. Part One gives a non-technical overview of the potential benefits and major pragmatic considerations of community currency projects. As such, it may be particularly useful for those in the policymaking world or people new to the field.

Chapter 1 discusses the rich and varied ancestry of complementary currencies, placing the subsequent sections within a historical legacy. Chapter 2 then turns to the objectives of community currencies and emphasises the importance of an outcomes-led approach to their design. We focus on four areas of impact that currencies often address: raising the quality of public services; supporting small businesses and the local economy; addressing social inclusion and building social fabric; and improving environmental sustainability.

Chapter 3 gives an overview of the kinds of stakeholders community currency projects typically engage with, and what levels of commitment and contribution can be expected from each. Some of the challenges associated with undertaking such a large, complex and multi-partner project are also discussed.

From here, Part Two moves on to consider the 'nuts and bolts' of currency design, delivery and implementation. Although this section is necessarily more technical, we hope that the material will be equally valuable and accessible to both unfamiliar and specialist readers.

Chapter 4 summarises the major considerations of designing a currency and – while emphasising that each community currency is unique – provides a set of guiding principles for any currency design process.

We then go on to discuss in greater depth some of the technical design features that community currencies commonly incorporate in Chapter 5. Moving beyond community currency design features themselves, in Chapter 6 we cover the wider challenges of making a currency project a success. A currency can be fantastic 'on paper' – so to speak – but without a sound organisational structure or secure funding channels, it can be difficult to get off the ground.

Chapter 7 focuses on developing an effective communications strategy, something essential for getting a currency project going and bringing the necessary people on board at each stage. Finally,

Chapter 8 covers the evaluation of a currency project. For both individual community currencies and the field as a whole, it is essential to build up a rigorous body of evidence in order to learn what works and what doesn't, which design features are effective – or ineffective – in different circumstances and how projects can be further refined and improved.

We have avoided overly specialised terminology, but a certain amount of technical vocabulary is unavoidable. We have included a glossary to cover all of the technical terms used – all entries are underlined in the body of the book for easy reference. The 'Further Reading' section includes books, publications and online resources for those wishing to go deeper into the community currency field.

Also included are a number of case studies of 'currencies in action'. With these we aim to make the book less abstract and give the reader practical examples so as not to get bogged down in the technicalities.

For easy reference, each currency case study is marked with one or more symbols indicating its major objectives. These symbols recur throughout the book and are detailed on page 24 and 25:

 Democratising services and organisations

 Supporting the SME economy

 Countering inequality and social exclusion

 Addressing environmental impacts

 CCIA currency

The index at the back of the book will help readers to navigate the case studies of over 30 currencies included, as well as further mentions of their features throughout the book. For more information on each currency, and the concepts and terms that surround them, visit our online resource: community-currency.info.

Though re-engineering money is no simple feat, we hope that these examples – and indeed the book in general – help to make currency design and implementation a more tangible, appealing and feasible idea for more people.

Key

Democratising services and organisations

Currency projects can be used to shift the balance of power within public sector and voluntary organisations, transforming the way their services are designed and delivered. A currency can help organisations explicitly value the contribution people make to their work, tap into underused resources in a local area or uncover the expertise of service users in designing the provisions to best meet their needs. This symbol indicates community currencies employed to these ends - projects that aim to improve and democratise the public infrastructure required for societies to thrive.

Supporting the SME economy

Many community currencies are designed to counter the dominance of large corporations through supporting more diverse SME economics and educating consumers about the choices they can exercise. Often part of a long term aim to support more jobs or livelihoods in a local area or particular sector, many of these currencies also seek to foster more sustainable business practices. This symbol appears next to currency projects aimed at supporting SME enterprises to these ends through a range of methods - for example by strengthening networks between independent businesses, providing alternative sources of credit, or enabling businesses to tap into their spare capacity and free up cash flow for essential costs.

CCIA currency

This symbol shows the six pilot currencies which were part of the CCIA project: Spice Time Credits, Brixton Pound, Makkie, e-Portemonnee, TradeQoin, and SoNantes. Stories and learnings from these currencies in action are included throughout the book; visit www.ccia.eu for more information and links to their websites.

Countering inequality and social exclusion

The networks and relationships of trust within a community form the basis of social life and nurture the ground from which the formal economy of money and markets grows. This symbol highlights the community currencies designed to bolster this 'core economy' - aiming to tackle some of the drivers and effects of social exclusion and inequality, and improve individual wellbeing. This may be, for example, by recognising and encouraging people's participation in local projects, supporting people with the necessary infrastructure to become active leaders in their community, or creating vocational or educational opportunities with those who might not otherwise have access.

Addressing environmental impacts

Community currencies play an important role in efforts to better value the planet's finite resources and incentivise more sustainable behaviour. Often working towards the high level objective of moving away from a money system that relies on endless economic growth, there are a number of ways in which currencies can influence this area. This symbol denotes the projects seeking to address a number of environmental concerns via a range of methods - such as rewarding waste reduction, mobilising investment for renewable energy or building public support for local supply chains.

Insight

Track this symbol throughout the book for quotes, terminology explanations and interesting examples of currencies making impact in their communities across the globe.

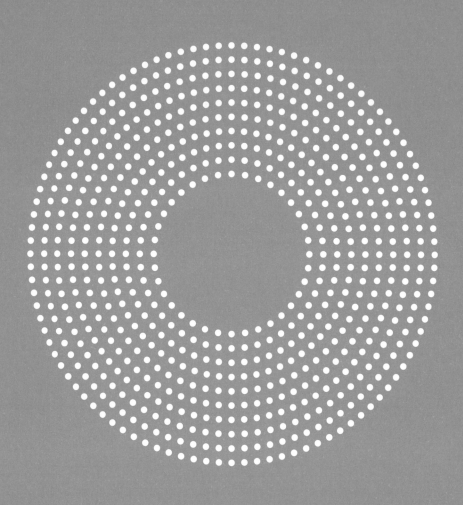

Part / 01

How can money better meet our aims?

For many, complementary and community currencies are fairly unfamiliar phenomena. The first part of this book is aimed primarily at those either entirely new to the field or still only loosely aware of the uses, aims and potential benefits of these pioneering monetary tools.

We present newcomers with the theoretical arguments and provide concrete examples of how and why various kinds of complementary currencies, designed as additions to mainstream money, have emerged over the years. By situating the book's later, more practice-orientated content within a historical legacy, we hope that the idea of creating new currencies will appear less strange to the reader. Through positing money – all types of money – as simply a tool designed to achieve certain objectives, we hope to empower readers to reconsider how money *should* – and indeed *could* – function better to suit society's needs.

01

Chapter 01

REBIRTH OF AN OLD TECHNOLOGY

Community currencies have flourished in recent decades. However, these contemporary projects have emerged from a rich historical legacy that continues to throw up new ideas and insights. Examining this legacy helps to demystify money – opening the way to new possibilities for its use and new designs better suited to communities' economic, social and environmental objectives.

In a recent Bank of England paper aiming to explain the nature of money, 'currency' is defined very narrowly and simplistically as paper notes and coins.[1] This, however, only makes sense when just one kind of money, in this case the pound sterling, is considered. To understand the practice and diversity of community currencies, many of which do not even come in any physical form, we need to think more broadly. By expanding the definition of currency – and by venturing further back into economic and cultural history – we can focus on the ultimately social role of money and consider new ways in which it can be designed.

From shells and giant stones to tobacco, clay tablets and grain, a huge range of media have functioned as currency. These include the variety of regional coinage used in the middle ages, the labour notes in the late 19th century and the many examples of scrip money used in the USA and Europe, particularly in the decade sandwiched between the World Wars and during the Great Depression.[2] Indeed, when thinking about money and currencies – what they are, what they do, where they originated – it becomes difficult to know where to draw the line.

Scrip money

Scrip money, or 'stamp scrip', refers to a number of paper-based complementary currencies that rose to prominence during the Great Depression, particularly in the United States, Austria and Germany.

Aiming to match unused productive capacity with unmet needs as the conventional money supply contracted, scrip money incorporated some form of 'demurrage', or negative interest. This required stamps to be purchased at regular intervals in order for the money to remain valid at face value, effectively decreasing the value of stamp scrip over time and thereby incentivising spending and discouraging hoarding.

The history of complementary currencies is complex and deeply connected to developments in society, social sciences and technology: indeed, in both forms and objectives, currencies tend to evolve alongside other social changes. As with much else, the history of this evolution is characterised by ebbs and flows, with recurring elements, rediscoveries and forgotten cases.

The broad category of *complementary* currencies – in other words, currencies that *complement* a dominant form – naturally requires the dominance of one, central, official currency to which all others appear as complementary. However, we should also shed the common assumption that contemporary economies revolve around only one kind of money. Dominant currencies have always and everywhere been supplemented by others.

Community and complementary currencies

Although often used interchangeably, 'community currency' and 'complementary currency' strictly refer to subtly different phenomena.

Complementary currencies are designed to sit alongside mainstream money to address objectives that the conventional money system can't.

Community currencies – the prime subject of this book – are a subset of complementary currencies that are tied to a specific, demarcated and limited community. This community could be, for example, geographical (local currencies); business-based (mutual-credit systems); or even online (digital currencies). As such, a community currency is designed to meet the needs of this defined community, typically on a not-for-profit basis.

In fact, what has been historically the case is still true today: many people use several kinds of currencies, formally and informally, in their daily lives. This is not only when travelling to foreign countries and changing between, for example, euros, dollars or pounds sterling, but through loyalty cards, shopping vouchers, air miles, online gaming credits – all are currencies in their own right, even if not commonly described as such. The plethora of currencies we interact with today – understood here as merely means of transaction – are numerous and varied.

Although the earliest forms of complementary currencies evolved in the 1920s, the specialised theoretical field of research into them was not established until the 1980s, alongside increasing practical experimentation.

Aided by an internet-connected world, general interest in and knowledge of currency design has been building consistently over the last thirty years, promising that this will become a more stable and systemic discipline in future. The formal study of complementary and community currencies is still at an early stage, however, and has only entered university and government departments very recently.

The publicity storm around Bitcoin has marked the most notable popular challenge to understandings of money and finance in recent years – boosting awareness of currency design more broadly. Indeed, the very existence of this book, the EU-funded project that produced it and, last but not least, each and every individual reading it, are all indicators of the increasing momentum of currency innovation today.

Alongside advances in information technology, there is a growing awareness of money itself as not being a neutral and fixed element in the fabric of society. This realisation opens the door to many new possibilities for addressing prosperity, sustainability and wellbeing through monetary design. We now discuss some of the main developments that have brought us here.

The historic legacy

The 'miracle of Wörgl'

The 1932–3 'Miracle of Wörgl' – named after the Austrian town in which it occurred – is one of the best-known examples of a community currency stimulating the local economy. In the midst of the Great Depression's monetary contraction, the town's new mayor, Michael Unterguggenberger, issued a town currency incorporating demurrage.

Currency circulation was boosted and the small town of Wörgl was able to stave off the effects of the global crisis: unemployment was vastly reduced; streets were repaved; new houses were constructed; major infrastructure projects were accomplished. All was financed by the town's 'free money'. As Wörgl's example gained fame, the Austrian central bank stepped in. Community currencies were outlawed and the Depression returned.

WIR Bank

The Swiss WIR Bank (abbreviation of *Wirtschaftsring* or 'business circle' Bank) was founded in 1934 as business was decimated during the interwar financial crisis. Today, the WIR Bank has a ten-figure turnover and over 60,000 members – mostly SMEs (small and medium-sized enterprises) in construction, hospitality, manufacturing and retail. The bank provides these members with credit at virtually zero interest, marketing opportunities and a clearing system, through which goods and services can be exchanged using the bank's own currency: the WIR franc, which is pegged at par but not redeemable with regular Swiss francs.

Shortages of national currency thus need not affect actual economic activity, with the WIR Bank having a countercyclical effect – that is, expanding during recessions and contracting during booms. This allows SMEs to survive and even prosper during times of uncertainty in the mainstream cash economy.

Some of the most commonly cited examples of successful currency schemes, like the 'miracle of Wörgl' and the WIR Bank in Switzerland, were founded in the first half of the 20th century and still inspire currency practitioners all around the world. The WIR Bank in particular, a business-to-business currency operated as a co-operative and supporting the SME sector, is often mentioned as a successful enterprise standing at the intersection of economic and social purposes. Its 80-plus years of operation and adaptation provide inspiration and encouragement to current currency designers; and it is in the lineages of such successful systems, past and present, that lessons can be learned and new technologies and ideas more readily embraced.

Modern grassroots origins

The modern history of community currencies truly began in the early 1980s with the advent of information technology and in response to the economic hardship of the 1970s. Michael Linton, in British Columbia, Canada, originated the currency concept of Local Exchange Trading Systems (LETS) and designed a networking computer programme to support them. Linton's software allowed community members to easily log and share their offers and wants, as well as record transactions between them. This innovative model took hold around the globe, most prominently in the 1990s. LETS have since become *the* flagship community currency for many.[3]

LETS (Local Exchange Trading Systems)

LETS today are essentially mutual-credit systems for individuals, rather than businesses. Members of a LETS advertise their skills and services and exchange these with other members in return for credits. LETS are intended to mobilise the latent capacity of a community by providing both a forum and medium of exchange outside the conventional market economy.

The networks are co-operatively managed and self-regulating and are commonly associated with the ideals of empowerment, localisation and community building. Unlike timebanks, they have no central broker and members negotiate prices for services, with credits normally valued on a one-to-one basis with national currency, rather than in time.

The growth of such do-it-yourself currency initiatives broke with the assumption that monetary and financial innovation was the exclusive purview of governments, or inevitably wedded to the needs and wants of corporations and banks. Instead, currency experiments started to be harnessed for the benefit of people, local businesses and their wider communities.

Within this bottom-up innovation, the first modern experiments with time-denominated currencies emerged at around the same time. Explicitly focusing on *social* exchanges, time-currency systems were popularised in the early 1990s by Edgar Cahn, who first coined the term 'time dollar'. Cahn anchored the practices and *ethos* of the ensuing wave of currencies on the values of solidarity, equality and respect. Timebanks and time-credits are the two types of community currency that most directly reflect these values.

Time-based currencies

The community currencies most widely used to recognise the value of activities neglected by the mainstream economy are timebanks. The principle behind such currencies is simple: one hour's work equals a unit of time. Exchanges between members are mediated by a broker, who matches the requests of one member with the skills offered by others. This offers an incentive for people to help other members of their community and can give isolated or economically excluded individuals – such as the elderly – the opportunity to 'buy' services they would otherwise be unable to afford and to feel that their own skills are valued and needed by others.

A second model useful for increasing social inclusion, which is a derivative of traditional timebanking, is that of time-based currencies often referred to as time-credit systems. Although working on the same principle of one hour = one credit, this model overcomes certain limitations of timebanks: most significantly, exchanges are not limited to being between individuals or by the mediation of a central broker. Instead, the currency – whether physical or electronic – itself mediates exchanges, circulating freely between any individual or organisation willing to issue or accept it.

While timebanks tend to operate in hyper-local geographic areas and are usually limited to members exchanging their skills with one another, a fully-fledged time-credit currency has greater potential to engage businesses and larger-scale community projects.

Both LETS and time dollars form much of the basis of present day community currency schemes, practised all around the world in networks of different sizes. There has not yet been a reliable census of all the systems in operation – in part due to the varying terminology used in different languages, as well as many projects' hyper-local focus, which means that systems often emerge and disappear quietly.

These grassroots currencies, launched by individuals and small groups of concerned citizens, reached new levels of significance when the 'trueque' community currencies in Argentina supported the livelihoods of up to 10 million people following the 2001 crash of the national currency, the peso. More recently, the euro crisis has prompted other examples of similar currency initiatives – like the TEM in Volos, Greece, and many others in Italy and Spain – that have thrown the question of currency pluralism into the political mix. While the TEM ('Alternative Monetary Unit' in Greek) hit the local markets and international news as if it were a brand new invention, it was not – as we have seen in this chapter. Efforts to design countercyclical currencies to fill the gaps when national currencies fail will undoubtedly continue.

Trueque

The Redes de Trueque (Barter Networks) evolved in Argentina in the mid 1990s in response to the economic crisis and collapse of the national currency, the peso. The network created a countrywide chain of community markets, which used their own currency, the 'Credito', to facilitate exchange of goods and services. Acceptance of the Creditos of other markets was voluntary, while overall administration and structure of both the network and currency was entirely decentralised.

While this, along with the largely spontaneous nature of its appearance, left the currency vulnerable to fraud, the trueques and Creditos allowed countless people to survive a severe economic crisis, with membership peaking at 2.5 million individuals across 4,600 centres in 2001.

Argentina's trueque networks demonstrate both the potential of community currencies to function as alternative mediums of exchange during economic crises and the need to develop more accountable and resilient networks in preparation for such an eventuality.

The new millennials

In the early years of the new millennium, another wave of innovation emerged with currencies like the Chiemgauer in Germany, Banco Palmas in Brazil, Berkshares in the USA and Transition Pounds and EKO in the UK. These systems are distinct in that they are backed by their respective national currencies – making them redeemable for cash if there are no suitable spending options. These currencies are supported with formal organisational set-ups and funding requirements more akin to voluntary-sector initiatives than grassroots interventions.

Environmental sustainability has also become an increasing driver for many currency projects. Examples such as the German Regiogeld and transition currencies strive to stimulate sustainable development, encourage environmentally friendly activities and reduce carbon emissions.

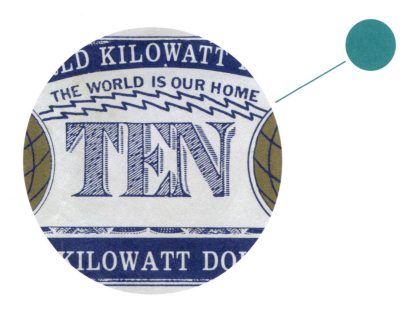

Regiogeld

Regiogeld refers to multiple community currencies across Germany, Austria and the Netherlands. As the name implies, 'regional money' serves a larger geographical community than most locally bound community currencies. They thereby increase the potential for environmentally sustainable production and supply chains by casting their net more widely across the local region.

While using a variety of models – including paper-based or electronic systems incorporating demurrage and some forms of local credit systems – Regiogeld currencies are designed to counterbalance the negative effects of globalisation through stimulating local SME economies. The most well-known Regiogeld currency is the Chiemgauer, operational in Bavaria since 2003.

Today's cross-sector fusion

Government and regulators have not always supported currency innovation – from the Austrian Central Bank's infamous closure of the highly successful local currency in Wörgl in the 1930s to today's lack of clarity, in many jurisdictions, on the tax and social benefit implications of LETS and timebank income (covered in Chapter 6). Such uncertainty can impede projects' collaboration with regulators or the public sector.

Conversely, however, some local authorities, city councils, regional governments and – most recently – the European Union have started to engage with and explore community currencies. This growing interest is largely thanks to the determined efforts of NGOs (non-governmental organisations) running currency schemes, who have presented strong cases to public funders to support such schemes. The backing of currency projects by public bodies offers not only a potential remedy for the many funding cuts that have ravaged countries since the 2008 financial crisis, but also an improvement to public services and policies beyond what money can buy.

CCIA launched in 2011 to demonstrate the potential of currency schemes to a transnational audience of policymakers, governmental agents and the communities they serve across the Netherlands, Belgium, France and the United Kingdom.

Several projects have since arisen with backing from local

authorities. The council of Lambeth in London, a CCIA partner, co-operated with the Brixton Pound to enable participating businesses to pay taxes in the local currency. Bristol City Council followed suit when the Bristol Pound launched in 2012, giving SMEs a broad chain of spending opportunities right from the start.

In 2011, the City of Ghent in Belgium rented out gardening spaces for a newly created social currency, the Torekes, which can be earned through many activities aimed at improving the built environment and community spirit of one of the country's most disadvantaged areas.

The city of St. Gallen, Switzerland, launched a time-credit scheme – the Zeitvorsoge initiative – to complement its ever-stretched pension and healthcare systems. The scheme allows people to earn and save credits by providing care services to elderly citizens. These credits can then be redeemed for care services in the future, when earners might themselves require assistance. Guaranteed by the city authority, this convincingly demonstrates how social-security systems can be bolstered without significant funding increases or reducing public services elsewhere.

The city of Nantes in France has mandated its public lending institution, the Crédit Municipal, to develop a currency for the city and its metropolitan region. Together with CCIA , the SoNantes was launched in 2015 as a ground-breaking regional currency model, providing interest-free liquidity for SMEs.

The SoNantes

Inspired by the Swiss WIR, the SoNantes currency launched in Spring 2015, supported with EU funding and managed by Nantes' public bank. Its innovative model allows businesses to trade using a closed-loop mutual-credit system, alongside individual consumers who have bought in to the scheme through purchasing credits for euros. These all-digital credits can be exchanged for goods and local services, including public transport, using a swipe card.

These examples are a new milestone for currency projects and, increasingly, specially designed currencies are being discussed as financial solutions for larger constituencies, with government bodies taking note of their benefits. There is an emerging demand for democratically determined economics that make the most of what money, as a tool, can offer – demonstrated by the dozens of proposals drawn up in recent years for a countrywide second Greek currency to allow it to stay within the Eurozone.[4] Complementary systems have been proposed to bolster, in a variety of ways, Greece's domestic market, which has all but collapsed under austerity measures. With the victory of Syriza in the general elections and new finance minister Yanis Varoufakis in post, ideas for a complementary currency have seen a renaissance in early 2015.[5]

Nation-states are, however, not the only big players to have opened their eyes to complementary currency models. Linden dollars (the currency of virtual world Second Life) and Bitcoin have been integrated into banking systems; large corporations too have initiated currency systems – for profit-driven purposes – such as Amazon Points, Google Wallet and Apple Pay. The rapid development of digital payment systems further demonstrates that money is a tool to be shaped and used.

In reality, money is simply a social technology and the ways in which it is designed, produced and controlled – far from being neutral or predetermined factors – all influence the effects it has upon society at large. Recognising this is the first step towards creating currencies as instruments for the benefit of particular communities.

Chapter 02

WHY – COMMUNITY CURRENCIES: MONEY WITH A PURPOSE

Community currencies can be employed to achieve a range of outcomes; here we provide an overview of their most common objectives.

From the complex history of and present-day experimentation with currency design that informs what is thought of today as money, we have begun to define community currencies as a specific category. They are distinct from other types of complementary currencies in two main ways:

1. Their explicit aim to support and build more equal, connected and sustainable societies;
2. Their design to be used by a specific group.

Often devised in response to the shortcomings of the monetary system – for example, the lack of credit available for small businesses, or funding cuts to public services – community currency projects set out in different ways to link up the spare capacity of some of their members with the unmet needs of others. Such currencies are broadly united by the aim of improving how money addresses the complex needs of societies.

Designed for impact

Starting from an idea of the positive impact a project would ideally have, well-designed currencies can address a wide number of different aims. Taking an outcomes-led approach is key to community currency design, ensuring that models are not created as ends in themselves, but instead as tools aiming to bring about a particular change.

Grouping examples of community currencies in terms of their intended impact is a useful starting point to compare how different approaches can be taken to address different issues. The following four areas broadly cover the social, economic and environmental objectives that inform the range of community currency projects operating across the world today:

1. Democratising services and organisations
2. Supporting the SME economy
3. Countering inequality and social exclusion
4. Addressing environmental impacts

Each currency model is in practice unique, tending to address several of the above objectives rather than sitting neatly under one category. To demonstrate the range and combination of existing currency models' aims, these four symbols occur throughout the book next to relevant currency examples.

Democratising services and organisations

In recent years, currency initiatives have become recognised policy tools for local governments. As monetary transactions are more and more prevalent in public service provision, people increasingly relate to these services – whether leisure, education or healthcare – as consumers rather than active citizens. Specially designed currencies can alter the dynamic of these increasingly monetised relationships, reinvesting them with social meaning.

Meeting community needs

Particularly since 2008, many states in Europe and around the world have taken political decisions to significantly shrink local government budgets. The needs of the communities that these budgets formerly served have not, however, disappeared. The shortfall created by a reduced public pot has given the rhetoric of citizens 'doing things for themselves' a new, politically loaded, significance.

When people are required to step in with their own time and resources to fill holes left by public funding cuts, inequalities become starker. Areas where residents tend to have more spare time and money are immediately advantaged over others. As such, cutting budgets with no provisions in place to keep social initiatives and key public services afloat has had a negative impact on community building. There are, however, more proactive steps that can be taken towards building communities with more active, empowered citizens.

As local authorities are pressurised into finding new ways to deliver services, growing numbers of currency designers are teaming up with forward-thinking public bodies to meet the latter's complex demands. Currency initiatives are practical responses to a range of policy areas that don't aim to replace or rollback public services, but rather to transform them into being more useful and better value for money. Though requiring significant upfront investment for lasting success, both in terms of economic viability and input from practitioners and end-users, community currencies can offer the long-term reward of a cost-effective tool that brings people actively into the process of solving the needs of their community.

A new way to deliver services: co-production

"Co-production is a relationship where professionals and citizens share power to design, plan and deliver support together, recognising that both partners have vital contributions to make in order to improve quality of life for people and communities."

from Commissioning for outcomes and co-production: a practical guide for local authorities [6]

Currencies can positively alter the relationship between public services and the people they aim to serve. In a public sector setting, co-production is increasingly used in the commissioning, design and delivery of services. Instead of trying to 'fix' people's needs, co-production looks at people's assets – their time, expertise and skills – and builds a more equal partnership to mutually design and deliver public services. This approach is opposed to – and indeed emerged as a criticism of – traditional, top-down and centralised models of service-provision, which see users largely as passive 'recipients'. As funding cuts put this model under increasing strain, co-production has gained the attention of policymakers as a possible alternative.

Zeitvorsoge

A good example of using a community currency to facilitate co-production of public services is the 'Zeitvorsoge' – literally 'time-provision' – initiative, launched and financed by the City of St. Gallen, Switzerland. Its main objective is to allow retired but generally fit senior citizens to save time-credits through helping those in need of basic care. Several local elderly-care organisations provide volunteers with opportunities to earn time-credits. The city itself acts as guarantor, ensuring that credits can be redeemed at any date in the future for similar care services if and when the earner requires them, either through the elderly-care organisations or peer-to-peer. This puts people in charge of their own care, allowing them to define and meet their own needs – crucially, however, with the professional and financial support of public institutions.

Community currencies offer a lever for realising the potential of co-production. They allow local authorities, professional organisations or businesses to explicitly value, and thereby incentivise, the contribution of the general public to their services. If well designed and implemented, a community currency can bring new ideas and inputs into public service delivery in a cost-effective way, strengthen independent community-based initiatives, recognise talents and activities not valued by the mainstream market economy and create their own dynamics of interaction and exchange.

People can be enabled to engage differently with care, education and leisure providers, such as health services, local council programmes, schools or charitable organisations. For instance, timebanks, in valuing people's time equally and incentivising schemes that encourage socially and environmentally beneficial behaviour, are prime examples of currency models designed to address this area.

Makkie

Introduced in 2012 in the Makassarsquare area of the Indische Buurt region in the Netherlands, the Makkie is a time-currency and loyalty scheme. Recently extended over a wider neighbourhood, the currency takes the form of physical notes, with one Makkie equalling one hour of service or community/voluntary work. Makkies can be redeemed for products, services, leisure activities or discounts at local shops.

The Makkie aims to empower citizens to take active roles in their community and increase residents' wellbeing. Activities are devised and supported by the local housing corporations, welfare institutions, professional organisations and municipality in response to needs highlighted by research and engagement with residents.

It is essential to emphasise that co-production is not a quick fix or an excuse for making individuals and communities unrealistically responsible for their own welfare; nor is it a silver bullet to the challenges of reductions in state funding. Although some of co-production's benefits can be easily monetised as direct savings to the state, many of these will likely be realised only in the mid- to long-term, while others (such as wellbeing or empowerment) can be hard to measure quantitatively.

Currency projects can enable councils to collaborate with other local stakeholders, such as independent businesses, residents' groups and charitable organisations. They are a tool through which constituents can knit together their resources *proactively* in order to strengthen a local economy and community, rather than *reactively* as councils are forced to do in the face of budget cuts. The broad aim in this scenario is to connect communities' excess resources, including the undervalued skills of its members as well as local facilities, in a way that better fulfils the needs and wants of that group and the wider community.

Supporting the SME economy

A diverse financial system catering to the unique needs of regional and local economies is essential for a healthy national economy. High streets containing a diverse mix of businesses form local economies more resilient to external changes and more rewarding for residents and visitors. Increasingly, these businesses are meeting the growing consumer preference for online shopping, forming what some have termed 'virtual high streets' of independent businesses to counter the current online big hitters such as Amazon and supermarkets' websites.

This desired state of commercial diversity is threatened by the mainstream growth model of the retail sector, which tends to follow the logic of 'bigger is better'. As well as putting local companies out of business, sprawling supermarkets and other large chains are most likely to leave an area in times of economic trouble, taking jobs and local amenities with them. However, with many large retailers recently suffering their worst sales figures in years, some are speculating that the bigger is better model could be coming to an end – increasing the chance for SMEs to regain their place in the market.

Currency systems can be designed to counter the dominance of large corporations through supporting the diversity of SME economies and educating consumers about the choices they can exercise. Some business-focused currencies assist businesses with operational aspects, such as purchasing supplies, incentivising sales and paying staff, helping them to improve productivity and become more resilient to changes in the wider economy. The target users of different models vary, with some business-to-business currencies aimed solely at SMEs and others extending to consumers.

Improving cash flow

Many European financial sectors, the UK's being a prime example, are dominated by a handful of international commercial banks. Because of this, they are easily criticised for being out of touch with the productive industries and SMEs that power regional and local economies. Since the 2008 financial crisis, banks have generally reduced lending to SMEs, leaving many businesses and start-ups in need of alternative credit sources.

Complementary currency initiatives can help SMEs support each other financially by lending and receiving credit, goods and services within the currency network – reducing reliance on cash and banks. For example, business-to-business (b2b) trade systems allow members to make purchases and sales using 'trade credits' or 'points', so they can reserve more of their regular cash flow for operational costs.

TradeQoin

TradeQoin is a Dutch SME trading network that lets businesses pay each other for goods and services with their own digital currency created at the moment of exchange. This helps members reduce their euro expenditure and offers SMEs fast and cheap working capital in TradeQoin. The online marketplace run by members stimulates business between participating SMEs.

Complementary currency systems have historically emerged as substitutes for mainstream money when there is not enough of the latter circulating. This can come in the form of increasing business cash flow, as has been discussed, but also as a replacement transaction medium when the regular option, for example the national currency, has dried up.

Bangla-Pesa

As a mutual-credit system for SMEs in an impoverished district of Mombasa, Kenya, the Bangla-Pesa allows members to trade goods and services with one another regardless of their conventional money supply.

Over 200 SMEs are currently part of the network, which itself is only one facet of a wider poverty-reduction programme. The currency was introduced by Koru Kenya, a local NGO working on economic relief and stabilisation.

As 75% of the SMEs in the area are owned by women, the Bangla-Pesa is also proving to be a useful tool for reducing both gender and economic inequalities. According to research carried out in 2014, the 'typical' network member is a 35-year-old mother who identifies herself as the main provider for 2-3 children.[7]

Creating strong business networks

Many currency schemes offer businesses an opportunity to form networks between themselves, providing a platform to publicise their work to the rest of the network. This can generate incremental sales from buyers looking for trade opportunities from within the currency network. Businesses can identify with one another over the ethical dimension in the trade they perform, or simply recognise the commercial advantage of increasing mutual exchanges. Currency networks can connect businesses with new customers sharing values such as reducing carbon footprints, or keeping production local.

Berkshares

BerkShares are the community currency of the Berkshire region of Massachusetts, USA.

The currency is purchased in return for US dollars at local partner banks, with an estimated 4.3 million BerkShares issued since 2006 and around 130,000 in circulation at any one time. The principle objective of the BerkShare, like other geographically bound currencies, is to keep wealth within the area and encourage localisation of production and consumption.

Furthermore, strong business networks encourage a self-help model of exchange and mutual support along supply chains. Through facilitating interactions between businesses, they encourage long-term relationships between SMEs in the same area or sector. This could be, for example, through building links between a service provider, such as a restaurant, and local suppliers, such as cash-and-carry or drinks companies.

Palmas

Banco Palmas is a community bank in Fortaleza, Brazil. Since 2000, it has offered interest-free microcredit loans in the local currency, the Palmas. The bank's objective is to localise production and consumption and, through the Palmas, retain more wealth within the area, generating both employment and income. Banco Palmas illustrates the benefits of a strong local banking sector for local economies, acting as a trusted backer of the community currency.

The example has now spread to over 100 locations across Brazil, and is acknowledged by the central bank as a valuable initiative.

Using spare capacity

Most businesses do not operate at 100% of potential capacity. The commercial benefits of connecting underused assets with unmet needs – a primary goal of complementary currencies – are clear. A reward currency scheme might enable businesses to exchange particular assets at reduced cost to loyal customers for points; or a trade network could provide otherwise underused services to other businesses in exchange for credit. For instance, spare cinema seats could be offered as competition prize or staff bonuses to another business, in exchange for credits. These credits can then be spent elsewhere in the network.

TradeQoin case study

Manoushka Botts, founder of Amsterdam-based CarCleaners.nl, is a TradeQoin member. Speaking of the benefits, Manoushka says:

"We have a number of cleaners on contract and during low season they have less work to do. I decided to start offering cleaning services in exchange for TradeQoin credit, which I can then spend on something I need for the business. What I'm looking for is a company or freelancer to help me develop a new website."

The TradeQoin network not only provides Manoushka with another source of income, but connects her to other local SMEs, supporting the area's economy overall.

Keeping money circulating locally

Pumping money into an area is pointless if it flows straight back out again. Yet this is precisely what happens with national or (regarding the euro) international currency. This leakage occurs because, if high streets are dominated by multinational corporations with non-local supply chains and there is no geographical restriction on where the currency can be spent, profits will not remain within the locality.

> "The SoNantes benefits those who produce and consume locally. It doesn't replace the euro, but provides an intelligent complement. It promotes local trade and short production and supply chains, allowing member SMEs to pay less in euros – helping them conserve their cash reserves. It gives each of us a new way to act for our region, for its development and for our jobs. It is a tool that we share so that everyone benefits."

Pascal Bolo, First Deputy Mayor of Nantes

Local currencies that are specific to a particular geographical area offer ways to keep more of the money in that area. They can help to plug the leaks – reducing the level of profits flowing to headquarters of large corporations, rather than back to the people that work for them.[8] Why does this matter? Because keeping money circulating within a locality or SME network, through wages or supply chains for example, increases opportunities to reinvest in that community and strengthens both economic and social local infrastructures.

Chiemgauer

The Bavarian Chiemgauer is the first and largest of Germany's Regiogeld initiatives. The currency incorporates demurrage, or negative interest: in order for Chiemgauer notes to remain valid at face value, a token must be purchased and attached every three months. This incentivises spending and discourages hoarding, meaning that the Chiemgauer circulates more rapidly and frequently than the euro. The 600 SMEs in the network meet around 50% of local people's needs. Around 2500 users and 250 voluntary organisations also use the Chiemgauer.

Eusko

The Eusko is a regional currency launched in 2013 in Bayonne, a city in the French Basque Country. As of October 2013, it is the largest complementary currency in France, with more than 466 business members, 2,300 individual users and 170,000 Euskos in circulation.

The Eusko aims to relocalise the economy through encouraging local trade; develop social ties and solidarity; better value the Basque language and culture; support local projects of common interest; and reduce the environmental impacts of the economy.

The Eusko is backed and valued one-to-one with the euro.

If a certain critical mass of businesses and individuals using a community currency is reached, then a mutually reinforcing relationship between benefits to local buyers and sellers should develop. As more local SMEs accept the currency, more individuals are encouraged to shop with them; local businesses then recycle community currency profits back through, for example, exchanges with other SMEs and bonuses to staff – using money that can then only be spent once more back in the local economy. A virtuous circle of spending and reinvestment is thereby created.

With production and supply currently so globalised, this ideal state is unlikely to be realised immediately. Community currency practitioners therefore actively identify and fill gaps in the local economy. One way to do this is to use national currency surplus – built up as individuals and businesses buy the local currency without redeeming it later – to make interest-free loans to sustainable local businesses that meet supply and production needs and gradually build a local economy that is both commercially and environmentally sustainable – and avoids leakage.

EKO

The EKO is the community currency of the Findhorn ecovillage in north-west Scotland. Pegged to pound sterling, it operates alongside the village's LETS to provide a strong and resilient local money system.

The EKO offers low-interest loans to various community projects. To date, these have included a youth project, a local co-operative and a community wind farm. A sustainable housing development will also soon be financed through the EKO. The currency contributes to the ecovillage's overall vision of demonstrating an economically, environmentally and socially sustainable community-based development model.

Educate consumers and increase customer loyalty

Currency projects can stimulate thinking and discussion about how money works and impacts a local economy. Raising people's awareness of the socio-economic dimensions of their consumer behaviour can have direct benefits for local economies through increasing custom to participating businesses. As customers chat to business owners about why they're participating in a community currency scheme, and what advantages it brings to both parties, stronger connections between local people and businesses are forged. This can create a more social high street, where business owners and customers get to know each other, as well as developing customer loyalty around the shared values represented by the currency. Both aspects can boost or stabilise the turnover of participating SMEs, as customers seek out participating businesses to spend their local money.

Local authorities, as major procurers of services and products, may be receptive to the benefits of community currencies. For instance, using a community currency to procure services is an active way to demonstrate support for independent businesses.

Brixton Pound

The Brixton Pound is a community currency operating in South London, UK. Although primarily designed to support local SMEs, the Brixton Pound also seeks to increase the sense of community cohesion and draw on the area's history of social activism.

Valued one-to-one against pound sterling, the Brixton Pound can only be spent with local SMEs and thereby aims to retain wealth within the community. Many participating businesses offer discounts to those paying in Brixton Pounds – in effect offering a loyalty scheme that both demonstrates their commitment to the local economy and increases custom. In the long term, increased links between Brixton-based SMEs themselves localise as far as possible supply and production chains to create a more sustainable and resilient economy for the area.

The Brixton Pound has demonstrated commitment to supporting independent businesses through vocal opposition to plans that would see many well-known local establishments evicted from one of Brixton's famous high streets: Atlantic Road. The high profile of the Brixton Pound helped the campaign gain media attention and draw 13,000 signatures on a petition protesting the evictions (the campaign was ongoing at the time of writing). This demonstrates how currency initiatives can situate themselves within wider communal, social and political life and the benefits they can bring to an area beyond monetary value.

Social highstreet case study

Research from the University of Bristol and Brunel University, London, provides evidence that community currencies primarily designed to support the SME economy may also have significant social effects. According to the research, transactions using such currencies – in this case the Bristol Pound – contribute to people making connections to others, to their communities, to the environments they move through and to what they consume, while developing feelings of trust and opening up new kinds of interaction. In other words, the conscious choice of businesses and consumers to conduct economic exchanges via a medium that explicitly values and supports the local area and SMEs can lead to significant gains in community cohesion and reconfigure social relations.⁹

Offer businesses and their customers new ways to transact

Currencies can provide businesses with point-of-sale options that they might not otherwise have been able to afford. A currency initiative incorporating digital systems, such as phone apps or pay-by-text options, allows participating traders to accept electronic payments – and offers customers new, often more convenient ways to purchase goods. Small businesses can thereby keep up with – or even move ahead of – the technology offered by large corporations, while the added convenience for customers can translate into a boost in sales.

Brixton Pound case study

Brixton Pound has pioneered new payment options for local traders. When the Brixton Pound launched their pay-by-text system, the added convenience prompted Alicia Reynolds – a Senior HR Officer at Lambeth Council – to request part of her salary in her local currency. In her words:

"It saves me a trip to the bank. Sometimes I'll go shopping, and then remember I don't have any cash on me, but then I realise, I've got my Brixton Pounds. Paying by text means you don't have to queue up and wait for change."

The success of pay-by-text spurred on a further advancement in 2014 – the introduction of 'tap and pay' technology with a corresponding app. The new system uses near-field communication (NFC) technology, which allows smartphones and similar devices to make radio communication with each other by touching them together or bringing them into proximity.

Evaluation of the Brixton Pound highlights the potential of community currencies to impact behaviour and affect attitudes. Of those using the currency, 70% reported that they had got to know local business owners better as a result, 55% that it had made shopping more convenient, 88% that it was good to be spending in a way that supported local values, and 82% that it had reinforced their pride in Brixton.¹⁰

Countering inequality and social exclusion

The day-to-day costs of active involvement in local voluntary or leisure activities are often overlooked. On top of major household costs like rent, bills or mortgage payments, the cost of, for example, taking a bus to another part of town, or paying a child minder, often prohibits people on low incomes from participation in local events. Volunteering at a primary school or helping to run a coffee morning involves time and money that not everyone has. By redistributing resources more equally, community currencies can help to overcome these inequalities of free time and money.

Social participation

Exclusion of certain groups from social life weakens community relationships overall. Specially designed currencies can be used to oil the wheels of social participation, ensuring that all groups are given realistic, relevant and meaningful opportunities to get involved in their communities.

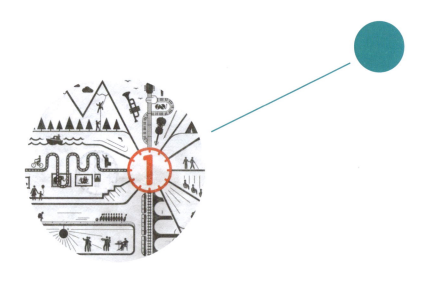

Spice Time Credits

Spice partners with local authorities, schools and housing associations to offer time-credits to individuals participating in voluntary programmes. Credits can then be traded between individual members – as in a traditional timebank – or spent at various non-profit, public or corporate partners. These currently include cinemas, gyms, family activities and vocational training. Spice also works with the public sector, utilising time-credits to introduce co-production to public services.

At both the earning and spending stages, one credit equals one hour of a person's time or organisation's services. The Spice system has its historical roots in the Welsh labour movement, when mining communities would contribute part of their wage to both support and access mutually owned local services, such as clinics, workingmen's clubs and libraries.

It is important to clarify that community currencies cannot single-handedly overcome the deep social, economic and political inequalities that exist within societies. These are structural issues requiring structural change. Nonetheless, well-designed currencies offer a unique tool for addressing some of the drivers and effects of social exclusion.

Involvement in voluntary and community work offers many benefits to the socially excluded and economically marginalised: a chance to develop new relationships, valuable skills and a feeling of self-worth. The work of such projects is also of great worth to the wider community, mobilising local residents' latent assets and skills. For example, credit-earning sessions allowing qualified but unemployed hairdressers to practise their skills and build up their haircutting experience also facilitate socialising. In this way, currency transactions can catalyse further community activity, as people think up new earning and spending opportunities for the currency system and form new relationships with local facilities, both private and public.

"The most exciting thing about time-credits is their diversity of applications. They can work with schools, social care, community connection, building social capacity. It can work whether you're a small or big organisation. They really allow us to improve our interventions."

Claire Mattison, Lancashire County Council, discussing Spice Time Credits

Moreover, the activities created through currency schemes give people extra incentives to engage with others in their area. If well designed, they can bring together a diverse range of groups: people from different generations, cultures, religions or social classes whose paths might not otherwise cross.

Makkie case study

The time-based Makkie amplifies the impact of around 250 community projects in East Amsterdam. A founder of a community transport service that uses the Makkie explains:

"Just going to the local market, to the hospital or to visit someone – those are the type of trips that pose a problem for the elderly. A taxi is too expensive and you have to order a ride with Connexxion [the local public transport company that offers trips for disabled and elderly] way in advance. Just getting dropped off for a small errand at the supermarket is impossible."

Now, she offers neighbourhood lifts in exchange for one Makkie. As a result, elderly residents are no longer house-bound and can travel safely to wherever they need to go – having a good chat on the way.

Supporting the core economy

The networks and relationships of trust within a community form the basis of social life and nurture the ground from which the formal economy of money and markets grows. However, as forms of unpaid work, the value of caring for relatives, raising children, assisting neighbours or carrying out household tasks like cooking, cleaning and managing finances, is generally not recognised in the formal economy. These ongoing tasks of maintaining and fuelling society and the lives that make it up, often but not exclusively carried out by women, constitute the 'core economy' – without which life as we know it would grind to a halt.

Much can be done to tap into, and strengthen, the core economy, as well as to better value and support it. Valuing here signifies the recognition of worth, of what this economy contributes and achieves, rather than putting a specific price on it. This is where community currencies can play a role.

Currencies based on time-exchanges explicitly recognise the skills of those making up the core economy. For instance, in a time-credit system, a neighbour providing respite care for a local carer can be rewarded for their time with a credit. This credit could then be redeemed for a school trip for their child or a trip to the local cinema. The idea is not to give volunteers a form of payment, as the activities themselves tend to be considered intrinsically valuable – in other words carrying them out is a reward in itself. Instead, time-credits are a recognition of the time spent in and for the wider community. They allow those carrying out this work to take up opportunities that might otherwise be inaccessible, or even donate their earned credits to local charities or vulnerable individuals.

Addressing inequalities

In any given society, certain groups are more powerful and better-off financially than others. Social policies that aim to enhance or 'grow' the core economy must therefore go hand-in-hand with measures to promote greater equality within and between different social groups. A systemic approach understands the dynamics of inequality: what the causes are and how they interact with and reinforce each other. Social and cultural factors such as gender, age, disability, ethnicity and sexual orientation influence the way people experience income and wealth inequality and often intensify disadvantages. Addressing complex systems of inequalities – both in economic and social terms – therefore requires specific strategies.

Community currencies cannot be expected to tackle these inequalities alone, but they do offer a valuable tool. Crucial to reducing inequality of any type is empowerment. Community currencies can help redistribute power from those who already have it, through wealth or other forms of privilege, to those who don't.

Spice Time Credits case study

Cheryl Hughes first earned Ely Time Credits through participating in community projects, getting her whole family involved to earn enough for an upcoming day trip. Participating in these activities helped Cheryl build new relationships and get to know new people locally. She then formed a new group herself: Community Mothers. Cheryl says:

"Time Credits opened my eyes. I never thought I would be able to do anything other than care for my children because of my dyslexia. It's helped me gain confidence in myself and improve the way I now live my life."

Empowerment and self-worth come hand in hand, and timebanks and time-based currencies that value a diverse range of skills and knowledge allow both to grow. The voluntary activities facilitated by a currency system enable participants to gain new experiences that offer intrinsic rewards, such as feelings of pride, but are also extrinsically valuable, as the skills they involve are widely applicable in the worlds of paid work and formal education. In this way, currency projects can directly address inequalities of learning, training and employability by putting those with less opportunity to gain the types of skills sought by employers on a more even footing with those who enjoy a more privileged status.

Improving individual wellbeing and health

Most people would agree that a successful society is one where economic activity delivers high levels of sustainable wellbeing for its citizens. In this context, wellbeing considers how people feel and function, and how they evaluate their lives. By providing opportunities for social contact and enhancing self-esteem, community currencies can contribute significantly to improving personal wellbeing.

Such projects offer avenues for socialisation and skill-learning to groups who, to varying degrees, may be excluded from the world of work. In these ways currency schemes can help reduce inequalities arising from high demands on service-provision in low-income areas – a strain that might arise because families with lower incomes have fewer resources to meet their own needs. Higher levels of wellbeing are often associated with positive outcomes such as improved physical health.

Feeling better

Independent evaluation of time-credit schemes run by Spice shows that participants feel fitter, report fewer health problems and visit GPs less often. In 2014, independent impact assessment of Spice found that:

- 65% of users reported a generally improved quality of life
- 45% reported feeling healthier
- 19% reported going to the doctor less frequently

These health benefits are likely knock-on effects of significantly increased levels of community engagement, which helps individuals to feel socially valued and empowered.[11]

Addressing environmental impacts

Human wellbeing also depends on a healthy environment. Community currencies play an important role in efforts to better value the planet's finite resources, move away from the doctrine of endless economic growth and incentivise more sustainable behaviour. There are a number of ways in which they can influence this area, such as rewarding carbon reduction by citizens and businesses or creating better accounting systems for the valuation of natural resources.

Incentivise sustainable behaviour

Redesigning money with ecological objectives in mind can drive behaviour and consumption changes that lead to energy saving, waste reduction, organic food production and more. A currency can, for example, function as a savings and reward system where credits earned through environmentally friendly activities, such as switching to a green energy provider or bringing domestic waste to the local recycling centre, can be exchanged for public services and environmentally friendly products. Other currencies can mobilise investment in renewable energy, whether at a household, corporate or state level.

e-Portemonnee

e-Portemonnee (E-Wallet) is an electronic savings and reward system designed to reduce household waste and support environmentally sustainable behaviour in the 44 municipalities of the East Belgian province of Limburg. Municipalities can award digital credits to residents for environmentally positive actions, such as switching to a green energy provider, donating goods to a local second-hand shop, or composting food waste. These credits, accessed through the participants' national ID cards, can then be spent on sustainable services and products, such as public transport, environmentally friendly household products or educational courses.

"Home composting, reduction of water consumption, switching to green power ... these are just a few of the many ways in which people can earn points with e-Portemonnee. There are people now who actively search for opportunities to earn and spend credits. And that's great, of course, because it means that with the e-Portemonnee, you can really affect people's daily behaviour, which means that the benefits will be long-lasting and more widespread."

Leen Frensen, Sustainability Officer, Diepenbeel, Belgium.

Value natural resources: linking money and nature

At global level, many argue for a stable unit of account that reflects the planet's natural capacities. Such a currency would not solely facilitate trade and pay taxes, as mainstream money does today, but also account for the finite natural resources that a monetised economy is based on. Rather than being excluded from economic decisions, as they often are today, environmental considerations could be 'priced into markets' through, for example, accounting for the renewable energy used to produce kilowatt-hours of electricity. This is an ambitious aim that would require top-down economic and monetary reforms.[12]

Terra

The 'Terra' is a proposal for a commodity-backed currency, proposed by Belgian economist Bernard Lietaer. Like other comparable models, the Terra is designed as an inflation-immune currency capable of stabilising global trade. This is achieved by linking the value of the currency to a 'basket' of around a dozen core commodities, such as oil, gold and copper.

As the value of these commodities rises (or, indeed, falls), so will the value of the currency, meaning that its 'real' value should remain constant in relation to the 'real' productive and commodity-based economy – that is, non-inflationary. The Terra is proposed as an international unit of exchange capable of providing businesses and states with a stable and shared measure of value regardless of wider inflation.

At local or regional level, energy currencies can promote more sustainable consumption and generate funds for investment in renewable energy production. These self-financing currencies could be redeemable in local participating businesses and, potentially, with producers of local renewable energy.

SolarCoin

SolarCoin is a digital currency incentivising the production and use of solar electricity. The technology behind the currency is similar to the better-known Bitcoin; however, as the name suggests, SolarCoin has a specific environmental aim. Producers of clean solar energy receive the currency on top of their feed-in tariffs for generating solar power.

Support sustainable business practices

Well designed and implemented community currencies encourage businesses to adopt more sustainable practices. This can be done in numerous ways, with different objectives requiring different types of currency.

Reward currencies can incentivise the purchase of more sustainable products among consumers: points earned when making a purchase can be redeemed as a discount the next time a sustainable product is bought. This in turn incentivises businesses to stock more of such commodities. Reward schemes can also target businesses or public institutions directly by providing access to growing networks of ethical consumers for organisations that switch to more sustainable practices, or incentivising public bodies to adopt sustainability criteria into their procurement processes.

Local currencies can encourage sustainability by tracing back through production and supply chains and encouraging potential local suppliers to join the scheme. This provides opportunities for businesses as well as consumers to spend locally when sourcing materials and products, reducing carbon emissions generated by transportation of goods.

Eco-Iris

The Eco-Iris is a local currency introduced in the Brussels region by the Ministry of Environment to promote sustainable behaviour and purchasing, boost the local economy and improve community cohesion. It is currently operating across five neighbourhoods. As with the e-Portemonnee in Belgium, members receive Eco-Iris for switching to environmentally friendly lifestyles or purchasing sustainable goods and services.

Local associations, shops and traders can also join, increasing spend options for members. Although not technically backed by legal tender, business owners may exchange excess Eco-Iris into euros at the Brussels Environment Ministry, at a discount.

This chapter has provided an overview of the most common aims of community currency projects. Turning now to the question of 'Who', in the following chapter we consider the roles of partners, backers and users – the motor of these people-powered money systems.

03

Chapter 03

WHO – CURRENCIES FOR THE PEOPLE, BY THE PEOPLE

Community currency projects are often inspired by strong principles and these are essential to their success; however, any currency design must keep the users' needs centre stage. Here, we discuss why the 'community' in currency design matters, what kind of partners and stakeholders currency projects typically need to bring on board, as well as their likely level of participation.

Community currencies are distinct from the wider field of complementary currencies – and indeed most other financial innovations – because they are set up with the involvement of the people and organisations that will ultimately be affected by them.

As such, community currencies are centred on the benefits to their users and stakeholders, beyond the purely commercial logic of 'more consumption for less money'. Typically, this means community currency projects will be established as not-for-profit initiatives. Even if they are commercial in nature, the benefits directly return to the wider community they serve.

Moreover, by recognising that all money is a social technology that rests, one way or another, on personal, economic and political relationships, community currencies not only focus on the individual as an economic actor, but also consider their position and aspirations within wider social and political networks.

Hence, the interplay between different stakeholders – including citizen groups, the public sector and businesses – becomes central to these unorthodox monetary projects. The projects only work if the operation of the currency involves the different participants who it is designed for. Since they are voluntary in use, community currencies will only be adopted if they clearly offer added value for all concerned. These benefits do not have to be monetary or financial – here all notions of value, including solidarity and community spirit count in the make-up of a currency.

Stakeholders in a currency system

The following section explores the different groups that feed into a currency's planning process and determine its success, often more so than the actual initiator or host organisation. To distinguish different interests and possibilities for collaboration, we have outlined three broad groups: partners, backers and users.

a) Partners

This group consists of organisations, individuals and entities that have direct interests in a currency's operation and are usually involved in the design, launch and operation of the initiative.

Effective and efficient implementation and running of a currency is always a matter of teamwork and partnership, requiring all partners with an interest in its aims, or who can help with the process, to be as involved as possible. Partnerships will differ, depending on the main goal of the currency, but it is these groups – be they local charities, independent business networks, university departments, city councils – who will offer invaluable insights into the needs and wants of users.

b) Backers

Backers provide financial or other support and are not involved in the implementation of the currency itself. A community currency's success will always be influenced by the support, opposition or indifference of related organisations. Funders and grant-providers, locally, nationally or at European level, might be crucial for the launch of the initiative. They will be particularly willing to support the currency if its goals are aligned with their own purposes.

c) Users

Last but not least, users are those who make the transactions and circulate the currency – whether as individual consumers, businesses or public bodies. The currency's acceptance by its intended users is what ultimately makes the difference between success and failure – not only in terms of operation and turnover but, more crucially, in terms of the expected impact of the project. As these initiatives are not designed to be an end in themselves, but instead tools to serve certain needs or interests, users' non-engagement would clearly indicate a disconnect between the initiators' assumptions and the community's real needs.

Currency users are never passive: all in one way or another shape the project. This group is a crucial component of the co-production process. They are not simply consumers, using the currency as a means of exchange, but 'pro-sumers', who take an active role in meeting communities' needs through mobilising previously underused skills and resources.

Levels of engagement

The following schema looks a bit more in depth at the roles different groups might play in a currency system – considering six levels of engagement. These vary depending on what role each party plays, how much resource they contribute and what benefits each stakeholder stands to gain:

- Leading
- Integrating
- Co-partnering
- Sponsoring
- Participating
- Championing

The levels are by no means static. For example, a stakeholder might initially champion a currency, and later become a participant by accepting the currency for their services. A consortium of stakeholders might come together to lead a currency – such as in the case of the Makkie in East Amsterdam, where the local authority shares responsibility with local NGOs.

Most involved: Leading a community currency or integrating it into daily operations

Leading

A stakeholder may opt to run the community currency, becoming both the lead operator and promoter. This could be, for example, a local authority, chamber of commerce or NGO. The lead stakeholder carries out the day-to-day tasks of running the currency, and is responsible for engaging users.

Makkie organogram

Amsterdam East local authority joined CCIA as part of a wider government effort to tackle inequality in the Dutch capital. With 24,000 inhabitants, a disproportionate density of social housing and high unemployment rates, the Indische Buurt region of East Amsterdam has been highlighted as an area in particular need of investment. The time-based Makkie currency has become an important tool for building social inclusion in the area.

Diagram 01 shows how the local authority collaborates with other partners in the running of the Makkie.

Integrating

At this level, a stakeholder may be significantly involved without actually running the project, instead integrating the currency into their systems. For instance, a local authority may pay contractors with the currency, stipulate usage of it in contracts, accept the currency as a form of tax payment or offer to pay staff members a portion of their salary in the currency. In this way, the currency becomes embedded into the council's procurement, social care and environmental policies.

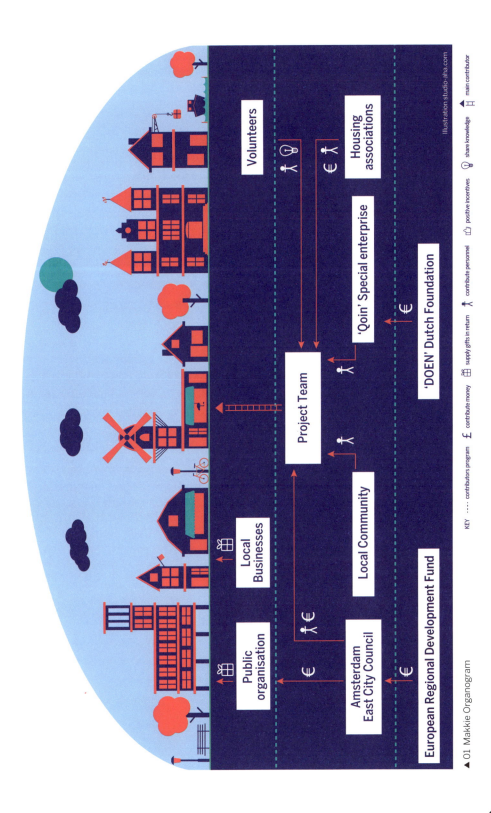

▲ 01 Makkie Organogram

e-Portemonnee organogram

Diagram 02 shows how the municipalities of Limburg support the implementation of e-Portemonnee through integrating it into their systems.

A business could integrate the currency into core aspects of its running – not only through accepting the currency in exchange for providing goods and services, but, where possible, through paying some staff salaries or bonuses in it, as well as promoting the currency along its supply chain and using it to buy goods. Such a business would be actively involved in the running of the currency and would have a say in its developments.

Less involved: Co-partner or sponsor a community currency

Co-Partnering

A co-partner would be an equal partner with one or more organisations committed to running the currency. A stakeholder at this level may not have instigated the currency, but can provide ongoing technical expertise for the project, such as ICT or fundraising. A co-partner could also provide administrative processes, develop or invest in training, or assist with performance evaluation. All of these areas are key to changing organisational culture and encouraging front-line staff to embrace the initiative.

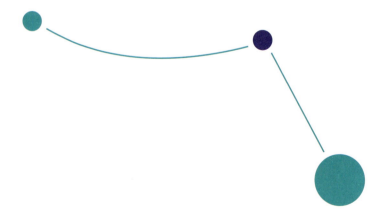

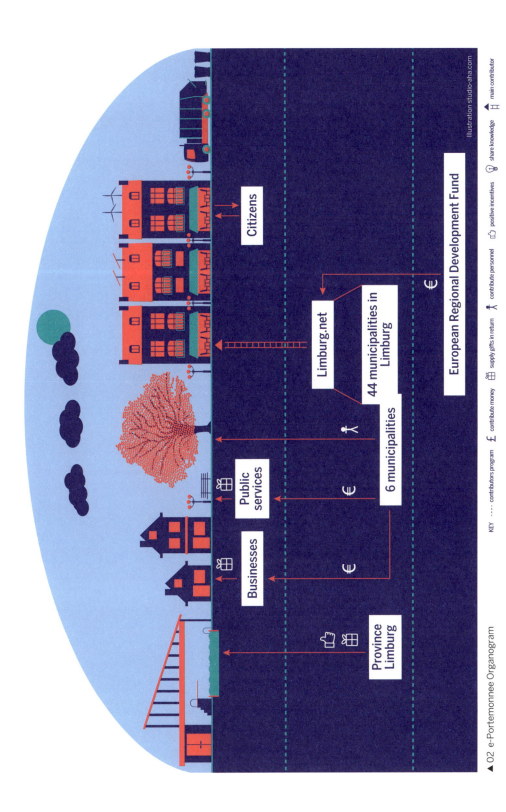

▲ 02 e-Portemonnee Organogram

Spice Time Credits organogram

Diagram 03 shows how Spice partner with public institutions such as schools, local authorities and housing associations, as well as charitable organisations to provide opportunities for participants to earn time-credits. Spice provides staff, training and support to allow partner organisations to set up their own time-credits systems.

Sponsoring

Sponsoring a group or organisation to operate a community currency is another way to be involved. Sponsorship is typically financial and may be part of an international fund or local grant. Stakeholders at this level may have a great deal of say over how the sponsorship is used and may regulate the currency, or may fund the currency to fulfil some of its local aims but otherwise remain at arm's length. Alternatively, a stakeholder such as a local business could sponsor the currency in a non-monetary way, by providing facilities such as ICT, space or materials.

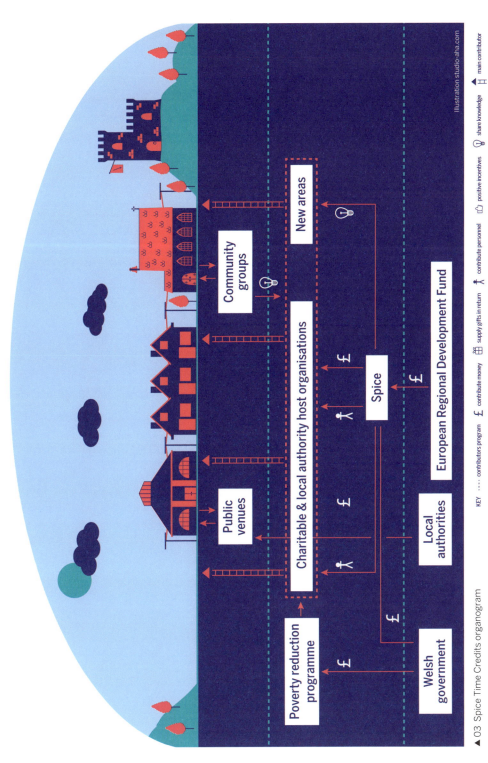

▲ 03 Spice Time Credits organogram

Indirectly involved: Participating in and championing a community currency

Participating

At this level, stakeholders are involved in using the community currency, without necessarily providing support or integrating it into their systems, but might issue the currency as reward or payment, or use it to buy supplies. A stakeholder at this level might allow residents or other businesses to pay for services in the currency without necessarily re-spending it – converting it instead back to a mainstream currency. Alternatively they might consider their involvement as a donation – providing excess capacity to the scheme as a conscious loss – for example by accepting time-credits for swimming sessions during quiet periods at a local pool.

Participation at this level provides important validation of a currency scheme, broadening the remit of spend options for users and instilling trust in the project.

The Bristol Pound and council tax

In March 2015, Bristol City Council became the first local authority in Britain to accept a community currency – in this case, the Bristol Pound – as a means to pay council tax. As well as representing a landmark for the community currency movement, the council's announcement essentially guarantees that anyone holding Bristol Pounds will always have a spending opportunity – everyone needs to pay council tax. Gaining this level of participation from a council helps hugely in building trust in a currency and establishing belief in its value.

Championing

Even if stakeholders do not want to directly participate, they can still offer support through championing the currency's use, lending support and validity to a currency without direct involvement. At this level of participation, stakeholders don't expect to gain any particular outcome from engagement with the project.

For businesses, this might mean hanging posters or stickers on their premises to raise awareness about the scheme. Public institutions could symbolically endorse the currency – as in the case of the Mayor of Bristol personally accepting his wages in Bristol Pounds, a move that garnered a lot of media attention. The Makkie received a similar boost through a visit from the Dutch Prime Minister, Mark Rutte. Political figures are often willing to associate themselves with projects they see as bringing benefits to the community. While falling short of the greater levels of stakeholder participation outlined above, such championing can secure valuable coverage for community currencies and help develop trust in the projects.

Challenges of a multi-stakeholder project

As currency projects often rely on a large number of stakeholders, establishing shared goals from the outset and developing a picture of how different objectives might interact can be difficult. A multi-stakeholder project requires ongoing consideration of each party's needs and proficiencies. Some of the challenges that can arise include:

Perception of risk

A large potential stakeholder may feel there is too much risk to get involved. For instance, a service supplier might show interest in a currency project's objectives, but not be comfortable with taking part due to its relatively unknown status.

Solution: Stakeholders could begin with a soft entry into the field, for example, through accepting a currency for procured services, with the potential to engage more in the future.

Slow decision-making

For example, the highly political environment and tight budgets associated with local authority engagement could stall the operations and decision-making process of a currency. Elections may mean a new administration, often with different aspirations and agendas.

Solution: This could be rectified by having a long-term and ring-fenced team working on the currency, able to mobilise funds and take some decisions autonomously.

Differing ambitions

Different stakeholders may have distinct ambitions for the currency. An SME might join a mutual-credit system to increase their turnover in the short-term, whereas those responsible for implementing the project would have a more long-term vision where the financial self-sufficiency of the currency model depends on members' continued trading.

Solution: A tight knitting-together of the skills and resources of the spectrum of stakeholders allows differing ambitions to be aligned collectively. A co-production approach can build or operate a project or service with an equal and reciprocal relationship between providers and users.

Co-producing a currency

The co-production method can be used in the currency design process itself to overcome some of the issues cited above. However, because needs, assets and objectives are unique to each individual and community, there is no definitive co-production blueprint. Rather, certain guiding principles should be considered. For example, within a currency project, co-production should involve:

1. Developing people's existing capabilities: Identify strengths and assets they bring to the table. Actively support people to utilise these at all stages of the currency project.

2. Mutuality and reciprocity: Offer stakeholders a range of incentives that enable them to work in reciprocal relationships with professionals and with each other, with shared and managed expectations.

③ Peer support networks: Engaging peer and personal networks alongside currency experts is the best way to transfer knowledge.

④ Blurring distinctions: Reduce barriers between professionals and recipients, and between producers and consumers by recognising that people are indeed experts in their own habits and needs – and, as such, in how a currency could align with these.

⑤ Facilitating rather than delivering: View the currency as a catalyst and facilitator of change rather than the central agent of change itself.

⑥ Recognising people as assets: See people as equal partners in the design and delivery of the currency, rather than passive recipients and burdens on the project.

These principles require the committed involvement of individuals and communities at every stage. A superficial application of co-production will be counterproductive. The potential rewards, however, are significant: people who are more engaged and involved in the currency project, a currency which is more responsive to its user's needs, and better and more cost-effective outcomes long-term.[13]

Currencies in action: E-Portmonnee

"Solar panels have always been popular here. The municipality used to offer subsidies to encourage people to install them, but the policy became a victim of its own success and, after a while, was not sustainable. So we started looking for other ways to incentivise environmentally friendly behaviour.

Talks were held with government environmental agencies and we consulted other municipalities to see if we could learn from their experiences. After a year of planning we announced the e-Portemonnee.

The system encourages a range of actions: reducing water consumption, switching to green energy providers through which people earn points. These can then be spent in a number of ways – on anything that makes it easier for people to act in a sustainable way.

e-Portemonnee is having a real effect on people's behaviour, rather than just a one-off or short-term impact."

Leen Frensen, Sustainability Officer for Diepenbeek, Belgium.

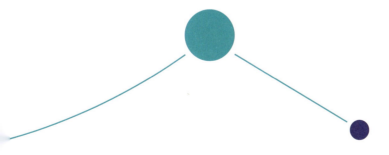

Part/02

INNOVATING MONEY — A HOW TO

We now discuss community currencies from a more pragmatic perspective. Covering the 'nuts and bolts' of currency design and delivery, this section will likely be of greatest interest to existing or aspiring practitioners, although anyone wanting a more thorough understanding of currencies is encouraged to read on. Along with detailed discussion of various community currency features, we cover the multiple challenges of taking a project from an idea to a reality, including the technical aspects of currency design and delivery, legal and compliance issues and developing an effective communications strategy.

Chapter 04

THE PROCESS OF DESIGNING A CURRENCY

Like any other complex project, a community currency's design is crucial to its success. This chapter discusses how to match a currency's design to its objectives, as well as the importance of integrating the needs and concerns of stakeholders into the design process itself.

Successful examples and inspiring stories from other currency projects can capture people's imagination, the media's attention and galvanise the energy and interest of many stakeholders for a new venture. However, and as much as these might serve as learning points to reach certain objectives, every currency in the world is unique.

This is not only because they bear different names, try to distinguish themselves in their communication and marketing material or use distinct software solutions, but because each currency is designed to meet specific needs in a specific context. This is true even if at first glance two currencies seem to be carbon copies in terms of their technical design elements.

People and the way they relate to each other, personally and economically, form the core of a community currency. From the beginning, the design process will need to take into account that the people involved in each currency will be different in their personalities, ambitions, needs and capabilities. These variations alone, multiplied by the many interactions that a successful currency project consists of, will ultimately lead to very distinct pathways, roll-out strategies and adaptations to whatever model might have served as the blueprint.

This lack of formula is not, however, a negative feature. Community currencies are all about providing adequate tools for people and organisations to realise their potential in ways that money as we know it cannot offer – therefore, their collective strength comes from their diversity.

As tempting as it is to draw up a simple linear guide to the stages of currency implementation, in reality no process is straightforward. Nevertheless, despite the lack of a transferable blueprint, every social initiative, currency or otherwise, should follow a logical progression from inception to implementation.

Non-linear

In order to provide openness and flexibility to the design, the planning and execution of a currency project is an iterative and adaptive process. A spiral, rather than a straight line leading from start to finish, more accurately describes this method of progression. This does not mean going round in circles, but rather consciously seeking to revisit certain core elements regularly, knowing they might have to be amended when other elements change, whether due to deliberate decisions or external factors.

In today's transient, diverse and increasingly virtual communities, people and the roles they are able to play are very likely to change during a project's lifetime. A currency will often start up with one set of people around it and be carried forward by a different group. In most cases, this also determines the character and details of a project.

As the process reaches the phase of design-refinement and approaches the crucial practical steps of piloting and 'learning from doing', many ideas, concerns, questions and feedback that have been discarded previously might resurface or become relevant to the final design. As such, it is always better to hear too many perspectives at early stages than too few.

The four core elements for any currency implementation process are:

1. participants – who?
2. their objectives – why?
3. functional design of the currency – what?
4. and finally, the organisational and practical necessities to making the currency a reality – how?

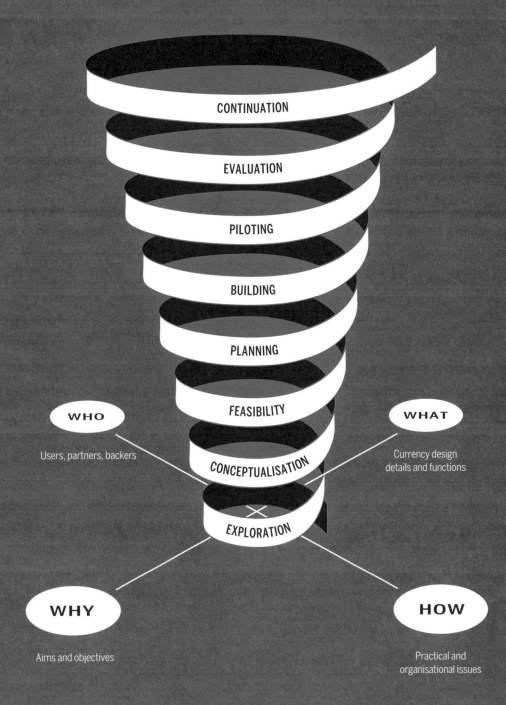

As a currency project proceeds through different stages of planning and implementation, these four core elements function like the cardinal points on a compass. The project's pathway revisits these points as it ascends, bringing improvements in the currency's design and final implementation. With each step forward, the overall project will have changed a little, with the four core elements mutually shaping, informing, enabling and limiting each other along the way. Each of the four can, in their own way, claim primacy over the other, yet none can fully define the others without being effected in return.

This is why we visualise the currency design process as a spiral continuously moving through the four cardinal points as it moves up through eight different stages in its progress, from planning to piloting and finally full operation.

Phase A: Planning

The first step is a market analysis, researching the socio-economic context and, if a currency is deemed feasible and useful, what the design of a basic, viable prototype might look like. Depending on the project's complexity and partners' and stakeholders' commitment, this phase might take from six months to two years.

Crucial elements at this stage are to clearly set out the goals and targets of the initiative and deliberate on the appropriate choices regarding the technical and operational set-up of the project.

Stage 1: Exploration

Exploring the needs, dreams and possibilities in a real context involves:

- Analysing the environment – how would a currency fit into the market?
- Identifying potential partners and stakeholders
- Testing ideas in various forums for support
- Sketching the general idea, working out goals and target groups
- Setting up a steering group and implementation team

Stage 2: Conceptualisation

Development of the concept of the currency and selecting the appropriate design (see Chapter 5) requires:

- Developing partnerships
- Producing presentations of the possibilities and early ideas
- Holding a 'theory of change' workshop to find out what all stakeholders want the currency to achieve in a context of what is feasible [14]
- Planning the intended impact of the currency

Stage 3: Feasibility

Several of the elements described in the following sections need to be explored in depth, to ensure that a no-go scenario is not discovered at a later stage.

All potential scenarios, good and bad, of the fully functioning currency need to be considered early on.

Stage 4: Planning

All elements from the above stages need to be combined and the implementation needs to be planned in detail.

Once an OK from the steering committee is granted and all the necessary resources are provided at the end of the stage, the project will progress to its practical phase.

Phase B: Building – Piloting

Acknowledging that any project of the complexity of a currency will always require testing and improvements, this second phase is about the implementation of a pilot. To allow for enough time for execution and testing of all scenarios, depending on the rate of uptake and intended scale, a further six months to two years should be allocated for this phase. Here all project elements need to be fully developed, and the currency will actually be launched.

Stage 5: Building

All operational elements now need to be set up for functioning. This includes the incorporation of an appropriate managing entity, signing of contracts and delivery against commitments.

This stage ends with the launch of the currency, whether in a protected beta environment or publicly, with sufficient provisions for potential changes stemming from the next stages.

Stage 6: Piloting

Finally, the currency is in circulation. From here on, forward data-collection and monitoring of the chosen key performance indicator is crucial.

During piloting, experience and feedback from participants and partners needs to be collected on a regular basis to understand the currency's strengths, weaknesses and developments over time.

Phase C: Continuity options

Once the currency is running, the immediate and long-term future comes into focus. The learning from the second phase needs to be considered and the course set for coming years.

Stage 7: Evaluation

Analyse the results of the pilot-stage monitoring. How did the currency function in relation to the initial plans? Can impacts for the users be demonstrated? Are they sufficient to justify further investment?

Can concrete bottlenecks or areas for improvement be identified? Here, all stakeholders need to be consulted, as this will determine the decisions of the next stage.

Stage 8: Continuation

For this stage, there are broadly four distinct options that depend on the findings in the evaluation stage:

Option 1 – Improve and innovate: Appropriate if the pilot shows that the currency has a lot of potential, but still identifies teething problems. Potentially, a radical redesign in terms of audience and purpose might have to be considered. Organisational or technological elements may also need to be adapted.

Option 2 – Scaling-up: A pilot phase usually takes place in a limited area. After a successful pilot phase, scaling-up might be possible and desirable. Existing processes are intensified and accelerated and, often, scaling-up means that the community currency will operate in a larger geographical area, or with larger groups of participants.

Option 3 – Stop: The community currency may appear to have insufficient support and does not reach its goals. Even if positive, impact assessment results might not be enough to justify further investment or effort. However, this option does not mean simply pulling the plug. Terminating operations is as sensitive a process as any other and requires solid preparation and strategy so as not to incur costs and losses for users and tarnish the reputation or potential of other currency initiatives.

Option 4 – Replicate: This option usually occurs only at a later stage and might be determined by other external groups. If the community currency has become sufficiently 'mature', it can be implemented with less effort elsewhere. Some degree of adaptation and innovation will of course always be necessary as no two contexts are exactly the same. This ensures great potential for direct and indirect learning for the initial currency project as well.

This chapter has presented certain guiding principles and advised a general mentality for currency design. The most important point is that it is essential to remember that currencies are tools to achieve specific goals – it is easy to forget this and start treating them as ends in themselves. An effective way to maintain focus on outcomes is to integrate the four 'cardinal points' (who, why, what and how) into every stage of the design process, revisiting them regularly as the project develops. The following chapter describes some of the most common elements of currency design in more detail.

Currencies in action: Spice Time Credits

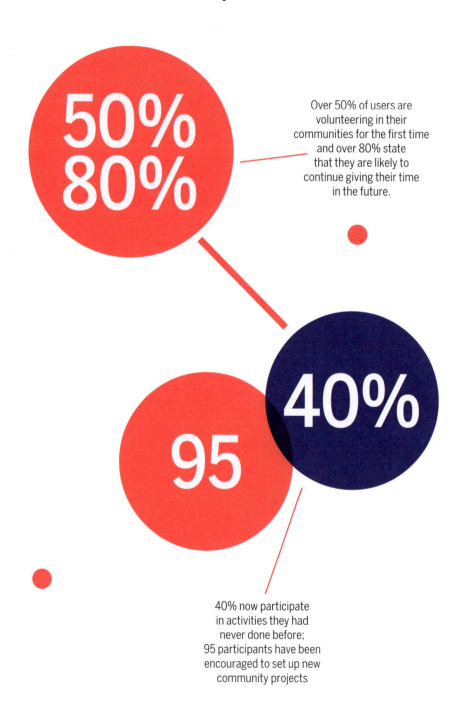

Over 50% of users are volunteering in their communities for the first time and over 80% state that they are likely to continue giving their time in the future.

40% now participate in activities they had never done before; 95 participants have been encouraged to set up new community projects

66%

71%

49%

45%

Increased levels of community participation are having positive effects on individuals:
66% say that Spice Time Credits have helped improve their quality of life;
71% have made new friends
49% feel less isolated
45% feel healthier since they started using Spice Time Credits.

Ref: http://www.justaddspice.org/our-work/scale-impact

PEOPLE POWERED MONEY

05

Chapter 05

WHAT – CHOOSING THE KEY FEATURES OF A COMMUNITY CURRENCY

Having discussed design in general terms, we now turn to specific features that can be incorporated into a community currency system. Each of them has certain benefits and potential drawbacks, so the choice of which to use will depend on which are most appropriate to the currency's objectives.

Function

Money is generally defined by the fact that it performs three functions. It acts as:

- a store of value;
- a medium of exchange; and
- a unit of account.

A community currency, however, does not need to be bound by this definition and can even aim for different functions altogether. Designing a currency involves looking at these functions individually and deciding whether or not, or to what degree, it should perform each of them.

Money as a unit of account represents a standard numerical unit of measurement and, as such, enables a uniform interpretation of value and cost. Without a widely agreed upon unit of measurement, money cannot be used to settle debts between different parties and effective price systems cannot be established – both of which are key elements of market economies.

In practice, only certain community currencies operate with their own unique unit of account, since it is hard to establish these in a voluntary environment with a large enough constituency of people. This means that many currencies stick to the national unit of account, typically with a straightforward one-to-one valuation, and only change the name of the currency unit – pound sterling, for example, functions as the unit of account for the Bristol and Brixton Pounds, among others. The units of account of various community currencies can be seen in **table 1** on page 103.

Money's function as store of value means it can be kept for a long time without losing its purchasing power. In practice, the extent to which this is true varies: the value of most types of money does fluctuate with time, typically diminishing as result of inflation or market demand. Complementary currencies almost never facilitate this function – with some even deliberately designed to prevent common practices such as hoarding. A popular tool for this is demurrage, which acts a sort of 'negative interest' rate that depreciates the value of the currency when it is not spent.

As a medium of exchange, money allows different parties to perform economic transactions beyond the limits of simple barter systems. Unlike barter, money overcomes what economists call the 'double coincidence of wants', which requires both parties to offer a specific good or service that the other desires. The medium of exchange function of money enables people to conduct efficient transactions and trade with each other without this 'double coincidence'.[15]

The majority of community currencies seek to act as media of exchange for the users for which they are intended. This tries to remedy the problem of money becoming more scarce in times of austerity or crisis – when the national money supply shrinks or when much of it accumulates in the hands of a few at the expense of the many – even though, in many communities, the capacities to produce and contribute on the one hand, and demand and needs on the other hand, remain the same. As an alternative medium of exchange, a community currency can connect supply and demand when mainstream money is scarce.

Denomination & transaction medium

As noted, community currencies have many different design features. One of the most basic of these is the 'denomination': the proper description of a currency amount, expressed through a range of different transaction media.

Denomination differs from unit of account in that it describes the quantities in which a currency can really be obtained – for example the currency's physical notes or coins. Unit of account, on the other hand, refers to the standard numerical unit of measurement that enables uniform interpretation of value and cost, such as dollar, hour or ounces of gold. This difference between the unit of account and denomination is best illustrated through practical examples. The Brixton Pound uses pound sterling as the unit of account, but it is denominated in B£. For the Makkie, the unit of account is time, and it is denominated in full and half hours.

Alongside any decisions made about the denomination and unit of account of a currency, the transaction media must be considered. It is in the field of transaction media that community currencies are typically more innovative then conventional currencies – and have introduced systems such as the Brixton Pound's 'pay-by-text', before many users of mainstream money were even aware of the idea of mobile payments. Typically, complementary currencies will use one or a combination of the following transaction media:

- paper notes
- coins
- tokens
- vouchers
- cheques
- 'show' cards (cards that must be presented at the point of sale)
- 'swipe' cards (card with a magnetic strip or chip carrying account information)
- 'smart' cards with various functionalities
- RFID (radio frequency identification) chips embedded in cards or other devices
- barcodes
- QR-codes
- SMS (short message service)
- Smart device apps

Bitcoin

Perhaps the most well-known complementary currency in use today, Bitcoin is a digital payment system. The first allocation, or 'mining', and consecutive transfer of coins is independent of any central authority or regulation. Bitcoins are transferred through a computer or smartphone without an intermediate financial institution.

As a currency it's simply a new medium through which to trade, operating under parameters such as the total number in circulation, the method by which new units are allocated and free-market pricing. Bitcoin payment systems use a decentralised ledger, which operates through a peer-to-peer network, to cut out the middleman role usually performed by a bank. This means the record of all transactions is not held centrally, but in a network of computers, which confirm the validity of new transactions using special encoding technology.

The table below gives examples of complementary currencies active in Europe and further afield, showing the range of media used to serve various functions.

Table 1: Community currency denomination and transaction media

Currency	Unit of Account	Denomination	Medium
Brixton Pound	£ sterling	Brixton £	paper, website, app, SMS
Bitcoin	Bitcoin	bitcoin, satoshies	electronic
e-Portemonnee	managed at par with 0.01 €	points	electronic, national ID as show card
Krugerrand	ounces of gold	Krugerrand	coin
Loyalty card	points	miles, points etc.	swipe card, websites, stamp cards
Makkie	time	hour, half hour	paper, website
SoNantes	euro	SoNantes	app, SMS, website, smart card
Spice Time Credits	time	time-credit	paper and online registry
Terra	managed price of commodities basket	Terra	electronic
TradeQoin	euro	TradeQoin	website, app
Ven	floating price of currency and commodities basket	Ven	website, app

Kruggerand

The Krugerrand is a South African 22-karat gold coin, available in denominations of half, quarter and a tenth of an ounce of gold. First minted in 1967 to help market South African gold, the Krugerrand has since become the most popular choice for global investors wanting to purchase gold. Unusually, the Krugerrand has the status of legal tender in South Africa, meaning that its units can properly be referred to as 'coins', rather than 'rounds' – the technical term for similar, non-legal-tender gold media produced elsewhere.

Loyalty cards

Loyalty cards – or, more generally, loyalty schemes – are marketing devices used by corporations to retain customers. They typically work by rewarding purchases with points, which can be accumulated and redeemed as discounts when making future purchases.

While not typically thought of as currency, loyalty schemes covering everything from cups of coffee to intercontinental flights do in fact have all the typical characteristics of currency systems. Currencies such as the Belgian e-Portemonnee pose the question that if these can be designed by corporations to meet profit-based objectives, why should they not also be designed by communities to achieve economic, social and environmental aims?

Issuance

There is no form of money that occurs naturally in any given society or community. Natural objects – from seashells and large stones to gold – have been used as money, but only when a society determines that they should be accorded a special status. The rules and processes by which these objects or units are turned into money are called issuance. This is what the central bank does when it prints on pieces of paper and then distributes them as banknotes, or what commercial banks do when they add numbers to someone's bank account when they take out a loan: they issue money into the economy.

There is some confusion as to the exact meaning of issuance, particularly with currencies that are printed on paper, because there can often be a lag between the time that a note is printed (when it is distributed to the issuance points) and the time that it is put into circulation by giving it to a person or business to use. To ensure clarity, three distinct properties of what is often referred to as issuance can be summarised as:

- the rules that govern issuance;
- the factors that will determine the quantity of money; and
- the mechanism whereby the money comes into circulation.

Within each category are a large variety of different methods and factors employed to manage and control the money supply.

The rules that govern issuance

The rules that govern how issuance will take place will be crucial to the proper functioning of the currency, and will in all cases be established by the organisation responsible for operating the currency. This does not, however, mean that these rules are always centrally created and simply imposed on businesses and users. Some currencies allow all members, for example in a co-operative set-up, to input into the design of the rules that govern the currency and its issuance. Others, like the Brixton Pound, do consult users and businesses, but use the operating entity to set the issuance rules.

The quantity of money

The management of the quantity of new money created, as well as the total money supply, is another area that requires consideration during the design phase. An example of a system that is carefully managed by the currency operator is the time-credits model pioneered by Spice in the UK. Under this model, the local Spice entities decide on the maximum amount of time-credits that can be distributed for an event or opportunity. This control over maximum issuance ensures that there are spending opportunities for all the time-credits issued, which is vital to the currency being perceived as valuable by its users. The time-credits are then issued when a person participates in the designated activity. This can be contrasted with the LETS and peer-to-peer timebanking systems, which both allow their users/members to issue units into circulation whenever their own balance is not sufficient to pay for activities or services rendered by other members.

SME businesses belonging to mutual-credit networks operate in a similar way, by allowing member businesses to create money in a fashion similar to overdraft facilities when they pay other members. Under these systems, although there are rules governing maximum negative balances for a particular user or business, there are no central rules governing the speed and point in time at which new money can be created or the total quantity of money that is circulating at a given moment. It depends rather on when and how much participants deliver and pay for each other's services.

Putting money into circulation

The final point to consider in regards to issuance is the particular mechanism that will be used to actually put money into circulation. In the mutual-credit example above, creation and putting into circulation coincide. Other options available are listed in **table 2** opposite.

It should be added that Bitcoin and other similar digital currencies are somewhat deceptive in their issuance, because there is no legal issuing entity. Instead, the rules are established by a predetermined algorithm. Although the total quantity of money as well as the issuance schedule is centrally regulated, the allocation of the next Bitcoins plays out in a decentralised fashion. None of these features are necessarily set in stone, however, as the governance model for Bitcoin has established that if a simple majority of the user community wish to, they could override or amend ('fork') any of the system rules. Such systems, therefore, have the potential to be fully decentralised.

Taking money out of circulation

To prevent inflation, alongside the issuance mechanism, the ways in which currency is taken out of circulation has to be determined. **Table 2** covers a range of different approaches to issuance taken by community currencies.

Table 2: Issuance

Currency	Rule setting entity	Management of quantity of new money and total money supply	Putting into circulation	Taking out of circulation
Brixton Pound	Brixton Pound CIC	Brixton Pound CIC and by users to the degree they want to purchase B£	When £ sterling is exchanged at designated change points or online	Only businesses can exchange B£ back to £ sterling
TradeQoin	TradeQoin, run as a co-operative	Member businesses	When businesses with insufficient balances pay another member	The sum total of all TradeQoin user balances is 0 at any time
SoNantes	Subsidiary of the Crédit Municipal de Nantes	Member businesses, Crédit Municipal and users.	For businesses SoNantes follows a mutual-credit mechanism Citizens obtain SoNantes by buying them for euros	The total balance of all SoNantes account holders will always be 0. Units purchased by consumers can be changed back to euros
Makkie	Consortium of 2 housing associations, Qoin and Amsterdam East council	Consortium with redemption partners	When a user performs a task for a partner organisation	Redemption partners return spent notes to Makkie consortium
e-Portemonnee	Limburg.net	Limburg.net and local municipalities	When they are claimed after a dedicated activity has been performed	Units being spent with the municipalities
Spice Time Credits	Spice	Spice with local partner organisations	Time-credits are created by Spice and distributed to the organisations offering volunteer opportunities to local people	Redemption partners return spent time-credits to Spice

PEOPLE POWERED MONEY

Backing

The narrow definition of 'backing' means that those holding the backed currency have a legally enforceable claim against the operator of the currency for a specific quantity of another currency or commodity. The usage of the term in community currencies often diverts from this (e.g. 'backed by services' in some Regiogeld or 'backed by the community' in some LETS), so it is more generally understood as the way of ensuring a minimal purchasing power (value) of a currency long-term by providing some sort of guarantee. In this way, the backing can be material (e.g. gold, silver or collateral), a different currency (e.g. euro, GBP, USD), or immaterial (e.g. a promise, collective consent, enforceable contract, government bonds or taxes). Whatever the specifics, the principle is the same: the currency is guaranteed to be exchangeable for a specific quantity of some other currency, commodity or service, and this guarantee gives it value in the eyes of the community of users.

Particularly when the backing comes in the form of a scarce resource, like national currencies or precious metals, the availability of that asset might limit the issuance of the currency. In community currencies, backing typically serves as a way to infuse trust in a scheme that does not have the endorsement of the government. The best known example of currency backing was the gold standard, whereby the governments of certain countries guaranteed a fixed exchange rate between a set amount of legal tender and gold bullion.

Community currencies that are backed by, and redeemable for other (conventional) currencies rather than a specific good like gold, are referred to as 'purchased and redeemable vouchers', of which Chiemgauer, Bristol Pound and Brixton Pound are examples. **Table 3** shows the backing methods of a range of different community currencies.

Table 3: Backing methods

Currency	Backing method
Brixton Pound	£ sterling in a protected trust account
TradeQoin	Member obligations to accept currency for goods and services and contracts with the operator determining the conditions of rebalancing their accounts when leaving the system
e-Portemonnee	Guaranteed redemption options by local governments
Loyalty card	Redeeming options with issuer, or with partner organisations
Makkie	Redemption guarantees of participating organisations and businesses
SoNantes	Like b2b barter but including public services like public transport, units purchased by citizens are backed by euros in trust
Spice Time Credits	Redeeming options with issuer, or with partner organisations
Terra	Stocks of commodities
Timebanks	Agreement by members to provide service at time parity
WIR	Collateral like second mortgages or Swiss franc assets

Design specifics

Although there are many different design features that can be included in community currency systems, we will focus on three that have a long history and can have significant impacts on how the currency operates. These features are demurrage or negative interest rates, bonus and malus conversion systems, as well as whether to require, allow or forbid the conversion of the currency into other currencies, mainly national legal tender.

Demurrage

Demurrage, in the complementary currency domain, is a built-in reduction over time of the nominal value of a currency. This discourages hoarding and incentivises spending by essentially levying a tax on currency holders. Ideally, demurrage should involve a charge of a simple negative interest, applied as regularly as practical. While this is easily done on a daily basis with electronic currencies, for paper currencies longer intervals may be necessary. In such cases, demurrage can be achieved by requiring the regular (monthly or quarterly) purchase of stamps that need to be put on the notes to maintain them valid at face value. With the value of the currency otherwise going down over time, it is in holders' interest to spend as quickly as possible, or before the next stamp is due.

Not every form of money is equally suitable for demurrage. Organising demurrage in electronic money is fairly easy, requiring only the application of simple bookkeeping techniques. However, as well as the potential benefits outlined above, demurrage has some drawbacks, which should be considered when deciding whether to incorporate this feature into the currency design.

Table 4: Pros and cons of demurrage

	Pros	Cons
Demurrage	Creates a clear disincentive against hoarding	Many people do not fully understand the concept
	Emphasises currency's main function: medium of exchange	Puts collective benefits over personal preference
	Nudges consumers to spend before having to pay fee	Goes against the common assumption about money – 'you gain money by keeping it'
	Enhances the velocity of circulation	Complicated in theory and practice, can keep businesses and individuals from joining

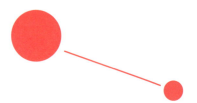

Bonus/malus

Bonus and malus in action

Until 31 December 2013 the Brixton Pound had a bonus of 10% for those who exchanged their pounds sterling into the local currency, meaning that £100 of national currency would buy B£110. Once in circulation the exchange rate between Brixton Pound and pound sterling remains at one-to-one: the bonus functioned as an encouragement to convert to and use the local currency. It also had a malus of 10% for those businesses who exchanged their Brixton Pounds into pound sterling. The malus functioned as a disincentive to convert and an incentive to find local suppliers to spend the Brixton Pounds with.

Within the community currency world, the term bonus refers to a premium paid to those who exchange legal tender for a community currency. Typically, bonuses take the form of a gift, issued in the community currency, added on top of the amount exchanged. Bonuses act as incentives to attract new users or to retain existing ones. Malus is the opposite of bonus – typically a charge on the conversion back into legal tender – and is a straightforward way of financing the bonus system.

Table 5: Pros and cons of a bonus and malus

	Pros	Cons
Bonus/Malus	Bonuses can encourage users to sign up to the currency	Businesses are discouraged from joining by the cost of conversion
	Incentivises the purchase of more community currency	Adds a layer of complexity to understanding the operation
	Incentivises businesses to find spending options for the currency they receive instead of changing back to national currency	Bonus can make the currency look like a commercial scheme
		Public sector partners might not be able to accept the malus and not participate in the currency
	Can generate income for the currency project or charitable causes	

Convertibility to national currency

Whether or not to make a community currency convertible into another currency, usually the national currency, is an essential question during the design phase. The decision will have major ramifications for the whole system, from the issuance process to the detailed legal requirements that convertible currencies have to follow.

The spectrum on which currencies sit can be illustrated by looking at how Brixton, Bitcoin and the WIR handle conversion of their currencies. At one end is the Brixton Pound, which states within the rules of the currency that all users and businesses may at any point convert any Brixton Pounds that they have in their possession at par for pound sterling.

At the other end is the WIR in Switzerland. Under the terms and conditions of the currency, exchange for Swiss francs, or any other currency, is not permitted. This is clearly stated in the agreement signed by all members and infringement can lead to exclusion from the WIR network. However, despite the prohibition and potential consequences in place, numerous users convert WIR francs into Swiss francs over the counter or though third-party platforms, usually for considerably less than their nominal parity of value.

Bitcoin inhabits the middle ground, leaving convertibility purely up to market demand. Many companies and trading platforms offer to convert legal tender into Bitcoin and vice versa. Interestingly the fact that conversion is not specifically prohibited means that regulators treat it as convertible and are starting to regulate Bitcoin exchanges rather than the Bitcoin currency itself.

Table 6: Pros and cons of convertibility and non-convertibility

	Pro	Con
Convertible	Guaranteed conversion can help businesses and users feel comfortable getting into the system Allows businesses to participate even if their suppliers are not part of the network Allowing conversion opens the possibility of generating revenue	Requires the maintenance of funds to meet conversion liability Requires compliance to financial system regulations Reduces the incentive, especially for businesses, to find creative ways to spend the currency or to encourage others in their supply chain to join the currency network
Not convertible	No legal tender reserves are required Closed-loop, non-convertible currencies operate outside financial regulation	Users and businesses can be more reticent to join such systems, especially if spending options are limited Requires active management of the volume of money being created to ensure that it grows in line with spending volumes

Security

A currency's physical and digital security is paramount to protecting its value, especially as the currency becomes more widely adopted and the likelihood of fraud, counterfeiting, and hacking increases. This is common in national currencies, but is also an issue in some complementary and even some community currencies, particularly those that can be exchanged for national currency.

Table 7: Anti-counterfeit measures

Countermeasures with physical currencies	Through accounting practices	Identity verification measures (for electronic transactions and membership)	In digital transactions
- Security papers - Special printing techniques - Registered serial numbers - Watermarking - Holograms	- Publicly accessible trading histories - Signatures or double signatures - Authorisation by different parties - Regular auditing	- Authorisation requirements by phone or electronic validation - Voice recognition, facial recognition, other biometrics - In-app security questions - PIN or passwords	- Password-secured user accounts - Chip and PIN technologies - Encryption (PGP, public-private key) - Third-party authentication

Market

The economist Hyman Minsky espoused the maxim that 'everyone can create (issue) money, the problem is getting it accepted'. Where mainstream money can be thought of as IOUs issued on the most part by banks as the legal tender to settle debts and taxes – community currencies cannot rely on legal rules to enforce their use. They are essentially voluntary in terms of participation and, therefore, need to encourage use by creating a viable and valued market. A currency's value is mainly achieved by ensuring it is widely and reliably accepted. It could thus be said that a complementary currency requires the creation of a complementary marketplace.

For this reason, the development of criteria governing whether to accept a particular business as a member of the currency network is particularly important. Some currency operators view any business wanting to join and willing to submit to the currency's terms and conditions as a good thing and welcome them, be it a McDonald's, major supermarket or petrol station. Others put lots of criteria on their membership, such as local ownership, provision or sale of environmentally friendly products and services, or being a small business.

A more open membership can make it easier to grow the network of businesses in which the currency is accepted and to ensure a good variety of goods and services can be bought with the currency. With a more restrictive membership policy, growing the network and ensuring variety become harder; however, the currency can gain from having a stronger identity, as well as potentially helping it to meet certain objectives, such as encouraging local shopping, incentivising ethical choices or favouring small businesses over large multinationals.

This chapter has covered some of the specifics of currency design in more detail. Combining this technical understanding with the advice on the design process in the previous chapter should help to ensure that currency projects are appropriate to their objectives, incorporating the right features, involving the right people and striking the right balance between clarity of purpose and flexibility of design. Rather than simply trying to replicate existing models that have been successful elsewhere, we hope that this will make it easier to focus on specific attributes of currency design and decide which are suitable and unsuitable for any particular context, community and goal. Next, we turn to the wider issue, far from specific to currencies, of implementing a long-term and complex project.

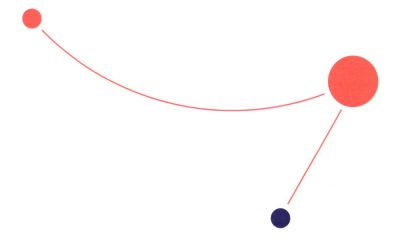

06

Chapter 06

HOW – IMPLEMENTING AND OPERATING A CURRENCY

The currency design itself is only one element of a much larger project. This chapter covers crucial questions about how this operates in reality – what kind of structure and financial set-up the team could adopt and what external expertise might be needed. Building on experiences of other currencies that have trodden these routes already, the chapter brings the key elements of an implementation plan alive.

Each individual currency is distinct. However, establishing a community currency is a project much like any other, although its core organisational, managerial and design features make it extremely complex, with more variables, more stakeholders but less best-practices and experiences than many other fields – and hence a greater possibility of getting stuck.

It is in the detailed planning and execution of such a project that the most ambitious initiatives also face their most severe difficulties. Often, the initial enthusiasm to do something radical and new obstructs hard-headed and careful project planning as well as the establishment of sufficient benchmarks and honest internal monitoring.

When deciding what kind of currency to create, there are concrete and often rather dull tasks that need to be kept in mind, as well as being budgeted. While designing the currency concept and convincing others to collaborate is fun and exciting, this is where often the hardest and least rewarding tasks await. This chapter covers the major components of this process:

- Organisational structure
- Finance
- Legal framework
- ICT applications

It is important to think about these tasks when building up a team and gathering expertise. Because many of these topics are equally valid for almost any other serious initiative out there, many other publications provide assistance with, for example, project management tools and processes. There are also expert organisations and consultants out there that can help with the overall process or specific expertise. We will therefore cover such aspects very briefly.

Organisational structure and governance

A currency project's organisational structure should reflect the values that the currency represents. Broadly speaking, this requires a governance structure that brings stakeholders together to participate in dialogue, decision-making, and the implementation of solutions to common problems or goals. This might follow the principles of co-production, ensuring that decisions are responsive to the broadest range of those who must bear the consequences.

Many of the currency case studies in this book illustrate the potential of projects to emerge from the bottom up. They often rely substantially on volunteers, or part-time staff based on short-term grant funding. However whether a currency emerges from a grassroots group in this way or is mandated through the routes of a local authority, developing sound organisational and governance structures is crucial for success and longevity – and to ensure that those giving their time are supported and recognised.

There are some key things to keep in mind when moving from an ideas stage and informal structure to a formal, incorporated organisational structure. These include:

- **Democratic decision-making:** Multi-stakeholder processes should enhance democracy within an organisation by increasing opportunities for those most directly impacted by decisions, particularly those at the grassroots who are so often voiceless in these processes, to effectively participate.
- **Flexibility:** Innovative projects like community currencies require a flexible operation in which small adaptations can be made at short notice. To make the currency a success, the set-up should allow currency professionals a certain degree of freedom, including a mandate to decide on activities and budget-allocation.
- **Transparency and accountability:** a multi-stakeholder process might involve consensus-based decision-making and operating in an open, transparent and accountable manner. As two of the central pillars of good governance, transparency is a necessary precondition for accountability. Without access to clear, accurate and up-to-date information, it is impossible to judge whether the standard promised by those ultimately in charge has been met.
- **Proficiency:** An organisation must stay operational throughout the process of design and implementation to assure stakeholders and potential end-users that the process has been well considered and planned.
- **Scale and scope:** Governance structures must suit the currency's scale of ambition. Small-scale projects might succeed in the early stages of devising a currency with less consideration given to formal organisational structures; whereas proposals for large-scale systems will need to formalise their structure at an earlier stage to, for example, secure funding or comply with regulations.

Typical forms of incorporation used by community currency systems in Europe include associations, charities, Community Interest Companies (CIC), co-operatives, B-Corp and limited companies. It is important to check which versions of these are available and to take advice from others in the field about the advantages of each.

Finance

Finance needs to be considered for two distinct phases: first, development and start-up activities; secondly, the need to sustain the network and systems put in place.

Although some currencies get started through the effective use of volunteers, sustainability usually requires funding. This ensures that all or part of the time people dedicate to the project can be compensated, as well as meeting the required costs for currency development. Funding can be drawn from users and stakeholders themselves, as well as institutions, foundations and local government.

To make the organisation of a community currency less vulnerable, dependency on one source of income is inadvisable. Subsidies, sponsoring, grants and a business model in which the currency itself generates income (e.g. registration fee, membership fee, transaction fee, balance fee) reduce dependence on one major funding source such as a local authority or charitable trust.

Sharing the costs

In 2014, Spice invited the organisations that had implemented time-credit systems to share with them the costs of carrying out an independent impact assessment. In return, these stakeholders received a well-researched report they can use to showcase their work, while Spice could afford to conduct a single, in-depth study, over a longer time period.

Business plan and budgeting

Before seeking funding, any currency will need a budget and business plan that establishes the costs that will be incurred in implementing, and then running, the currency. Some of the most common cost items are listed below, broken down into start-up and ongoing costs. Running costs are particularly important to bear in mind when devising a business plan, as the durability of the project could be determined to a great extent by how much resource is available for daily operations in the early stages of implementation. Some costs are a matter of choice, such as the extent to which the project will draw on external expertise either in the establishment or running phases.

Table 8: Costs to keep in mind

	Getting Started	Up and Running
Staff costs	Wages or expenses of development and operations team	
Office costs	Office space and equipment costs: rent, overheads, telephones, computers, printing.	
Communications	Hosting a website, designing and printing of publicity materials, producing and sending press releases, audio-visual equipment and software licenses.	
Administration	Opening bank accounts, establishing the legal structure, insurance.	Recurring costs: renewal of insurance policies, bank charges, hosting of website.
Experts	External expert costs such as ICT specialists, lawyers, currency design consultants.	Training of team members and partners.
Equipment	Purchase of one-off equipment for currency transactions such as payment terminals.	Maintenance and development of payment infrastructure.
Production	Design and production of notes, payment cards or other transaction media.	Adaptation or proliferation of transaction media.
Publicity	Engagement activities and launch event.	Ongoing engagement, educational and promotional activities.

Raising funds

Just like conventional money systems, community currencies' operational costs require sustained funding. The running costs of mainstream money often go unnoticed as they are built into the financial system as a whole, with mechanisms such as bank service charges, subscription for accounts and penalty fees raising funds to maintain operations.

Financial sustainability requires bringing in sufficient revenue to sustain the necessary personnel and administrative operations. Typically, currency systems need to cover at least a portion of their running costs in national currency, to establish a cash flow beyond the system's own currency. These revenues are typically generated from any or a combination of four sources:

1. Public and private grants
2. Donations and gifts
3. Fees paid by business and individual users
4. Secondary revenue options like leakage or selling advertising

Although, especially in the initial stages of the project, it is important to devise ways to generate income from the top two sources – grants and donations – ultimately the third and fourth sources should raise enough revenue to meet the operational costs of the currency. In practice, the financial sustainability of currency systems is often one of their biggest challenges. The drive to reduce any possible disincentive to use a new currency means that fees to businesses and users are often minimised. Indeed, the majority of community currency systems do not impose fixed costs on network members.

As systems mature, however, they need to start to raise more funds – be it purely in national currency, the complementary currency, or a mix of both. **Table 9** outlines revenue sources raised from currency users.

Table 9: Pros and cons of financing mechanisms

Financing Mechanism	Pro	Con	Example
Membership fees	Can be a source of regular income	If too high can be a disincentive to join the currency	RES applies membership fees for businesses, operating on a graduated scale of up to 500 euros per annum
Exchange fees from the community currency to national currency	Raises money when converting out of the currency	Can put off businesses from joining the currency	Brixton Pound formerly applied a malus of 10% for businesses changing B£ back into pounds sterling. This feature was dropped in 2014 to avoid deterring businesses from taking part
Transaction fees (for electronic transactions)	Raises regular money due to actual expenses occurring and matches the current transaction fees in the conventional money system	Not attractive for the person having to pay the fee (customer or business)	TradeQoin participants pay a transaction fee of 10% for purchases within the network. Part of the money generated from the fee is used to support a security fund to cover risks associated with potential bankruptcies
Advertising space (newsletters, website, app or note design)	Cost-effective advertisement opportunities for member businesses aimed at customers seeking to spend	Requires businesses to already have some degree of trust in currencies, whether through prior use or an inclusive and open design process	Beki raised over 12,000 euros from advertisements on the currency's paper notes
Demurrage	Encourages spending of the currency while raising revenue	Unless very large volume in circulation, revenue raised is limited. Not viewed positively by users and businesses	The Chiemgauer in Germany requires holders of notes to purchase stamps on a quarterly basis. For the e-Chiemgauer, the fee is deducted from balances automatically

Merchandise	Good way of raising awareness of the currency while raising revenue	Like any other product for the market, risk is involved: if it doesn't sell, you lose money	Brixton Pound sells branded merchandise as well as collector edition note sets
Leakage (units leaving circulation when acquired by visitors or collectors, or once a note has passed its use-by date)	The backing of these units in national currency won't be redeemed and so can be released for other purposes	Can be complex to administer and is only safe if it is known exactly how many units will never be redeemed	Chiemgauer notes expire after two years. After they have expired, the value of the national currency put aside to back them is used as additional cash flow for the project

RES

The Belgian RES aims to boost the local SME economy. Primarily a closed-loop payment system, the RES can also be bought by individuals in exchange for euros, at a discount of 10%. This model provides a complementary medium of exchange for both business-to-business and individual-to-business transactions. As of 2012, more than 5,000 businesses and 100,000 consumers were using the RES system, with an equivalent of €35million-worth of transactions conducted through the currency in 2011 alone.

Beki

The Beki is a regional currency operating in the Redange canton of Luxembourg. Valued one-to-one with the euro, the Beki is designed to stimulate the SME economy and transition towards environmental sustainability. To use the currency, businesses and individuals must become members of 'De Kär' – the organisation managing the Beki. Although redeemable for euros, Bekis exchanged back for the conventional currency incur a 5% charge, intended both to provide income for the operation of the currency and further incentivise spending in Bekis rather than euros.

Legal & compliance

Community currencies need to comply with all the applicable laws in the country where they operate. A number of areas need to be considered, depending on the specifics of currency design and implementation.

Space does not allow us to delve into the legal intricacies for every country and every type of currency system. As such, this section provides an overview of the most important areas to consider when starting a currency.[16]

These include taxation, social security, financial regulation, data protection, insurance and potential issues around public bodies' acceptance of complementary currencies.

Taxation

Tax authorities and regulators may consider community currencies to be a means by which individuals and companies can escape the tax implications of their transactions. It is therefore vital that any project seeks to mitigate these concerns by addressing the impact on any sales taxes, corporation tax and income tax obligations of the individuals and companies using the scheme. It is advisable to conduct research into the tax implications of any community currency, within its relevant jurisdiction, to ensure that currency users comply with the law.

Currencies with a predominantly social focus (e.g. timebanking, LETS etc.), due to their relatively limited scale in terms of individual balances, earnings and spending opportunities, in general have a low risk of tax avoidance by users. In closed-loop payment systems and legal tender-backed currencies, however, the potential risks are higher due to larger money flows, more members and procedural complexities. For these types of currency, measures need to be implemented to ensure businesses and users are fully aware of their obligations under the law, in terms of how transactions carried out in the system should be reported to tax authorities. In addition, the operating entity must understand the tax implications of their own activities and how to manage them.

In general, VAT should be applied to all transactions carried out in a community currency where (1) the activity occurred within the normal course of business activities and (2) the currency is convertible, either through a fixed exchange rate or a peg to national currency. This would not, therefore, include transactions conducted between individuals, as opposed to businesses, nor does it apply to transactions carried out in non-convertible unpegged currencies – both of which are therefore potentially exempt from the need to apply VAT. In all cases where VAT is applicable, it must be paid in the legal tender of the country where the currency operates.

The general position with regard to corporation tax is that all activity in a convertible currency or a non-convertible pegged currency should be included in the figures reported in a corporation's tax declaration. The position with regard to non-convertible unpegged currencies is more nuanced and requires further analysis.

The impact of personal income tax is very variable, depending on the system and the country. In most countries non-professional earnings are tax free and professional services are taxed no matter what was accepted in payment (national currency, community currency or in kind). However, in the Netherlands, for example, the adoption of LETS-type community currencies was helped by an explicit ruling that set the threshold for enquiring into the nature of a service being professional or non-professional at an annual equivalent of €3,000.

Social security and employment

One of the main target groups for social currencies is those not actively engaged in the economy; as well as vulnerable people, such as those with disabilities, unemployed people and people in deprived communities generally. Many of the people that could participate in a social currency scheme receive government welfare or unemployment benefits. It is, therefore, important that a dialogue is started and rulings are obtained from relevant national and local authorities on the potential impact of participation in social currency programmes. In some cases, such as for timebanks in the UK, tax authorities have issued official statements confirming that a certain level of participation in such systems will not impact benefit payments. In most cases, however, there are no official rulings. As such, working closely with local organisations with the required knowledge is crucial.

There is also a growing trend, especially with legal tender-backed currencies, to pay individuals in the currency. It is, therefore, vitally important to consider how this impacts on employment contracts.

Financial regulations

Any organisation printing physical 'money', often legally classed as vouchers, issuing electronic monetary units that are convertible into legal tender, or involved in the provision of payment services will need to review how the relevant financial services regulations apply to their currencies and which enforcement bodies (central banks, national and international financial regulators) need to be engaged for compliance or exemptions.

All countries have very strict laws restricting who can print money, and currency operators must ensure that they do not contravene these rules. In Germany, for instance, an old law is still in force that completely bans the printing of anything resembling money. Most other countries permit this, as long as steps are taken to clarify to users that these are not equivalent to legal tender notes. This can be achieved by calling the notes 'vouchers', adding an expiry date or giving the currency a name and look very different from the national currency.

The Payment Services Directive and the E-money Directive are two relevant pieces of European legislation, although their application varies widely throughout the EU. Some authorities, such as in France, have sought to clarify how community currency operators can comply with the law, while others have provided little guidance and are waiting for cases to emerge. In general, however, these regulations do not apply to non-convertible currencies.

France has carved out further exemptions by stating that any paper-based currency is outside of the scope of the Payment Services Directive, provided that no change is given for purchases and that only businesses are allowed to convert out of the currency. It is unclear whether any other European countries will follow this reasoning.

The E-money Directive is especially relevant to electronic community currencies. But again, interpretation and application differ widely. In France, for instance, the regulator does not consider complementary currencies to be within the directive's scope, since it was established with the intention of regulating prepaid payment cards, where money is stored on the card. However, most other countries consider electronic convertible currencies within the directive's scope and require the currency operator to obtain a licence.

As an alternative to currency operators obtaining a licence themselves, they may partner with an organisation that already has the required authorisation to run the currency. For instance, the

Bristol Pound collaborates with the local Credit Union, which already has the required E-money license.

Although complex pieces of legislation, both directives have an exemption for systems that can show they operate only in a 'limited network' both in terms of geography and variety of goods and services. Different countries have different interpretations of this exemption and its application varies between the UK, France and Belgium, where it has been tested so far.

Insurance

Insurance is relevant in two key areas: first, insurance relating to the currency's impact on users and volunteers engaging in work on behalf of the currency operator; secondly, how the governance board will be indemnified against major risks.

In some municipalities, citizens engaging in volunteer work are covered by a municipal (accident/disability) insurance policy. There are, however, many municipalities where this not the case.

Companies, charities, foundations and other entities (either profit or non-profit) seeking to introduce a currency scheme will need to consider the issue of potential liability of governance board members in the case of default, bankruptcy or other eventualities. For insurance companies, the risks involved in running a community currency scheme may not be straightforward to assess, which means complex negotiation may be required to agree upon the appropriate, cost-effective insurance policy.

Data protection

Data protection is important for most network services. Currency operators are responsible for formulating and implementing privacy policies to protect sensitive user data. The required safeguards for the protection of individuals are embedded in several legal texts.

Public sector acceptance of community currencies

Acceptance in lieu of legal tender, particularly by public entities, is a goal of many community currencies. Municipalities' acceptance of these currencies for both services (swimming pools, public transport) and taxes (business rates, local taxes) gives these currencies greater use, value and credibility. However, especially in the Eurozone, those trying to establish such spending possibilities in different countries have encountered barriers of different kinds, sometimes of a personal nature (risk averseness) and sometimes allegedly due to regional procedure regulations, state law or even EU law. It is advisable to check and clarify this with the relevant local institutions on a case-by-case basis.

ICT

Recent diversification of communication technologies, alongside the growing use of internet-connected portable devices, has begun to revolutionise the world of payments and finance. Though this seems like a step into a new future, most money in the world has already existed in electronic form for decades, with physical cash constituting only 3% of money in the UK and the remaining 97% being merely digital numbers that represent bank credit.[17] In the world of community currencies, this digital revolution has already been embraced, with the use of physical notes increasingly rare for many systems.

Computers have already been employed for some time to keep a central record of all transactions, including in small-scale currency projects, providing, in essence, an electronic registry and clearing system. In a second wave of currency projects, websites have become an efficient central communication channel for community currencies, informing existing and new members about the projects, events and notifications. Increasingly, currency websites include features like online blackboards that act as virtual marketplaces for products and services.

User friendly web platform

QoinWare is an IT platform developed by Qoin as part of the CCIA project. Building on existing Cyclos software, the platform adds further functionalities and user-friendly design features and incorporates bank-grade security. Qoinware and its earlier versions are used by a number of community currencies for electronic transactions, including TradeQoin, SoNantes, the Makkie and the Brixton and Bristol Pounds.

Analogous to the development of the Web 2.0 – that is, websites using technology beyond static pages and allowing user interactions – community currency web applications today allow more and more payments to happen digitally, without admins and accountants required to record transactions.

Online social networks, smartphones, near-field communications (NFC) chips, SMS gateways and, last but not least, cryptographic technology such as that used by Bitcoin are examples of digital developments that offer a wider range of possibilities to enhance the payment and social-facilitation functions of community currency projects.

ICT in action

Applications should contribute to the ease of use, efficiency and effectiveness of community currencies. Often, they are cheaper than non-digital solutions (such as printed notes or even coins) and can offer solutions for:

- **Membership management:** registering members, storing member information, analysing statistics on user composition.
- **Providing a marketplace:** connecting supply and demand,

recording transactions, making payments, tracking account activity.

- **Impact assessment:** monitoring and reporting of activity, extracting data from the payment function, surveying users on their experience and other data collection.
- **Financial management:** budgeting, forecasting, auditing.
- **Communications:** hosting a website and social media platforms to communicate with participants, using members' databases for newsletters.

ICT checklist

There are several specialist software platforms for community currencies available today, some simple, others with more sophisticated features. Use the following checklist when deciding what technological features are appropriate:

- **Accessibility:** can all users access it? For example, is it limited to smartphone owners, or can it be used across a range of devices? Consider how to tailor platforms to the needs and capabilities of users with disabilities.
- **Appeal**: is the user interface well designed and does it appeal to users?
- **Compatibility:** is it easy to connect to other elements of an ICT system, for example social media platforms or point of sale (POS) systems? Is it compatible with and does it support non-digital features of the currency operation, such as stakeholder earn-and-spend log books?
- **Compliance:** does it comply with laws and regulations?
- **Cross-platform options:** does it run on different operating systems on different devices (PC, tablet, mobile phone) and with different browsers?
- **Flexibility:** is it flexible enough to adapt to alterations made to the currency model?
- **Functionality:** does it offer all the options needed for the user?
- **Management:** can it be easily managed and does it have sufficient administrator functions?

- **Scalability:** does it allow a lot of users to transact at one time?
- **Security:** is it susceptible to abuse, malware or hacker attacks?
- **Stability:** is it reliable and error-free?
- **User friendliness:** is it simple, fast and efficient to use?

Depending on the kind of project (a small social program versus a large program linked to a national currency), the systems need to be less or more secure, which can add extra cost and processes for participants and operators.

It is not necessary to own the ICT infrastructure for the payment platform. This can drive up the cost, particularly if a lot of customisation is necessary, and is not always very efficient. Some common and open-source content management systems now include transaction modules that can be set up for community currencies (e.g. the Drupal CMS) or are offered as hosted packages (e.g. by Community Forge in Switzerland).

Even simpler is creating a user group on an existing platform (CES or communities.cyclos.org). These different options can be combined for a staged approach from quick and simple piloting towards implementation and adaptation at scale, building the systems up as the project grows.

CES

Community Exchange System, often referred to as CES, is a global, digital complementary trading network. More specifically, it is a community-based exchange system that provides an accounting system for its users to exchange their goods and services, both locally and remotely. Launched in South Africa in 2003, it can be thought of as a version of Local Exchange Trading Schemes (LETS) or mutual-credit systems, with some of the CES community currencies operating as timebanks.

Despite exciting developments in how ICT can today support currency operations, too narrow a focus on this during the early stages of project development can cloud the fact that successful initiatives depend on much more than the operating platform. Though a functional and bespoke ICT system is an often necessary component of currency operation, it is not sufficient alone for success.[18]

Currencies in action: Brixton Pound

"It saves me a trip to the bank. Sometimes I'll go shopping, and then remember I don't have any cash on me, but then I realise, I've got my Brixton Pounds.

I regularly shop at Faiz grocery shop and would normally buy yam, banana, plantains, and other Caribbean products. As a regular customer you get to know the market traders, and I can pay by text without having to wait for change.

People are always so curious when I pay by text. What service is that, they ask, and I explain

how it works and show them the Brixton Pound sign in the shop window."

Alicia, a Senior HR officer at Lambeth Council, London describes the added convenience the Brixton Pound provides, prompting her to request part of her salary in the currency to spend at local shops.

Chapter 07

THE IMPORTANCE OF GOOD COMMUNICATIONS

Like any other project, a community currency requires a professional communications strategy to succeed. Here, we cover the main points such a strategy will need to consider.

A key part of communicating a currency's message is education – it is important to take on the challenge of translating the basic ideas of how the currency will operate to potential users as early as possible. Desired users may well have never heard of community currencies, or may have different understandings of what it is they do. To get them on board, therefore, it is important to successfully demonstrate why the currency is worth using – and this is no small task.

Target audiences

When designing effective communications, the first thing to think about is the intended audience. There are several groups to consider when planning how to start publicising the project – for example, potential partners, local decision-makers and eventually journalists. But currency users themselves should be at the forefront of the communications strategy.

Primary audience

Users of the currency: This includes the individuals, businesses, public services and any other stakeholders that will circulate and transact in the currency. As these are the people and groups who will determine the success or failure of the project, this audience should be considered at the forefront of all communications planning.

Secondary audiences

Local influencers: Local figures can act as champions of a currency. Communicating well to them can provide exposure for the project, as well as legitimating the currency through its association with these trusted voices.

Policymakers & local government: Align messages with local constituents' hopes and ambitions and the policy goals of councillors that represent them. In the long term, support from policymakers in local government could be crucial to overcoming regulatory hurdles to the scaling up of a currency.

The wider public: People living outside of the reach of the currency might nevertheless engage with and disseminate stories of its development. It is important that this group is considered after the direct currency users; if the currency users are engaged and well informed, spreading a positive message to wider audiences will be easier. In this regard, traditional media channels such as broadcast media, radio and national newspapers are indispensable, but it is important to remember that over-exposure in the media can produce unrealistic expectations that in the long run alienate potential users. The level of media coverage should be proportional to the reach, capacity and aims of the project – local publications, online blogs and industry magazines are all good places to start.

Academics, community currency experts and practitioners: Academics and those already working in the community currency field can bolster the research ground of the project, providing evidence and legitimacy for its potential impact. Maintaining a presence in these circles is useful for gaining insights and advice. It is not usually necessary to actively contact this group – once the project gets going they will, no doubt, be aware of its developments.

Key messages

As a starting point, it is helpful to develop a clear message about currency initiatives in general, that embodies the project's values and can be conveyed to a broad range of audiences. For example:

"Community currencies are an exciting tool that empower citizens"

The next stage is to develop tailored messages, specific to the model and aims of the new currency, and to align these with the interests of the target audiences. Different aspects of the project will interest and appeal to each of the key audiences. Think up concrete examples that can accompany the message such as in the following table.

> "Having worked with the e-Portemonnee, my first piece of advice to future practitioners would be to develop an effective communications strategy. Just getting online and waiting for people to find you is not enough – you have to be proactive. This can be a slow process, but your communications strategy should aim to create a dynamic environment that 'converts' more and more people to your cause."

Leen Frensen, Sustainability Officer, Diepenbeek, Belgium.

Table 10: Tailoring messages to different audiences

For individual users	For businesses and traders	For policymakers and other influencers	For media commentators
Community currencies …			
offer a practical way to do something positive for your community improve community cohesion and can help preserve the cultural identity of an area	help you appeal to new customers offer interest-free lines of credit offer new resources such as IT facilities that are often cheaper and easier to use than regular accounting or e-payment technology	help people engage directly with the delivery of public services to improve quality represent a proactive step in improving cohesion between businesses, service providers and citizens	are an exciting new technology that can challenge traditional ways of thinking about money are a bottom-up solution for society's frustration with international banks and finance
Make it tangible with an example…			
Users say that pay-by-text allows them to get to know the local traders on a first-name basis	Small businesses can accept electronic payments from customers where previously they were only able to accept cash	Students from the local college can earn credits by helping elderly neighbours learn computer skills	Tired of rebuffs from the banks, a business network creates its own type of money

Get the message out

Developing a clear message and a timeline for milestones will make it possible to use a range of often free or low-cost tools, both online and offline, to communicate effectively.

Materials and visuals

Logo

A well-designed logo will prompt stakeholders and currency users to take ownership of the project and proudly promote it. The more meaningful the name or logo to the currency and the end-users, the more it will be remembered.

Transaction medium

The designs of a physical note, coin, swipe card or mobile app serve as powerful tools for what is often people's first encounter with a community currency. Physical notes, coins and swipe cards are handy for press photo opportunities and giveaways and a good-looking digital interface ensures that the website gets shared online. Investing in the design and material of physical transaction media – if issuing the currency in this way – is important in giving the currency the aura of 'moneyness'. Cheaply printed or poorly designed notes and coins are less likely to be taken seriously by users, whose belief in the currency is central to its success.

Print communications

Fliers, brochures and posters should be designed to appeal to all stakeholders, from local residents, to currency partners, SMEs and policy makers. Print communications should not overload people with information, but instead spark an interest that leads readers to the website or an event to find out more. Ensure digital versions are available for online dissemination.

Infographics

Graphic visual representations of information, data or knowledge are great for communicating how a currency system works to its potential users. The following graphic from the SoNantes currency is a great example of how the circulation route of a currency can be depicted in a clear and simple way.

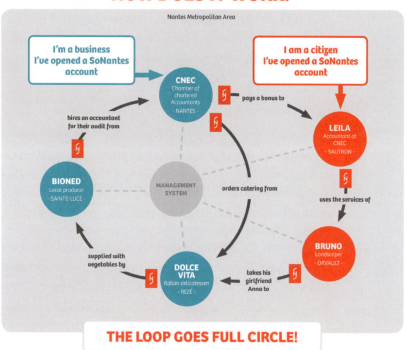

Online

Website

As a principal way people learn about a currency project, the website should appeal to all audiences. It should be easy to use, a place where questions about the project can be answered, supporters can sign up for newsletters and digital currency users can access their accounts. For currencies incorporating this latter feature, it is best to have visually distinguished areas of the site for user accounts and general information.

Social media

Communicating via social media is an inexpensive way to reach potentially huge audiences. It is important to identify the best social media platform for each message – for example, Facebook works well with images and videos and Twitter is good for striking up conversations. Take a tone that reflects the currency's values and remember to *be human* – people are more likely to engage if posts are not just promotional but offer honest, interesting and shareable content.

Videos and podcasts

Video interviews, podcasts and animations are effective in explaining the processes and mechanisms of a currency. They provide good content for the website and boost social media sharing among followers.

Canvassing, meetings and events

Digital communications media, such as those listed above, are highly effective in reaching young audiences and partners in the business, third-sector or governmental worlds. However, if aiming at social inclusion, the currency's audience is likely to include many with low incomes and other excluded groups, such as elderly people or recent migrant communities.

For different reasons (income, skills, language), these demographics are likely to be less capable of accessing online resources. As such, face-to-face contact through workshops and printed material in appropriate style and language are key to successful communications strategies. CCIA partner Spice, for example, distributes fliers and brochures in Welsh as well as English, so as to engage older time-credit users whose first language is the former.

Face-to-face meetings are therefore crucial to communicating about a currency project. They foster trust and build strong relationships with stakeholders and users. Many people won't have heard about community currencies and may perceive them as a complicated topic. Conferences and workshops provide good publicity and a chance to educate and engage people actively in the values and aims of the project. Capture feedback and contact details where possible – so it is possible to stay in touch with interested participants, perhaps sending a summary of how the event went and details of future actions planned.

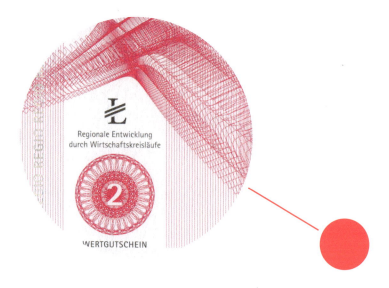

Press and public affairs

Press coverage

Local newspapers and neighbourhood circulars are good routes for alerting potential users to a project. Send out press releases in advance of all milestones and events to proactively attract media coverage. Be careful not to attract too much media attention too soon; overexposure of the currency while still in the early stages can give a false impression of its scope, generating unreasonable expectations and leading to disillusionment when these are not met.

High-profile supporters

Influence policy and gain publicity by engaging with politicians who have values and party goals in line with the project. Local councillors have a vested interest in the potential community benefits of currency projects and their attendance will raise the profile of events and provide photo opportunities. It is not usually necessary to focus resources on winning support from politicians: once a currency gains backing from its community, politicians will be keen to engage as well.

Attracting spokespeople

Identifying supporters, building a steering group and managing relationships are all key steps towards creating the operational community of a currency. Draw up a database of potential project partners and supporters of all levels of engagement, categorised by what role they could play – e.g. spokespeople, businesses accepting the currency for its services, councillors with a network of local contacts.

Initial approaches to interested parties should take the form of a conversation, showing where there is room for ideas to be incorporated. Currencies depend on the engagement of stakeholders and for this they must feel like they are listened to. A transparent approach is key to reminding potential partners that this is a project with a set of values that they can align themselves with.

Maintaining a network

As well as raising awareness, communications strategies need to consider how to build and maintain a network. This network will include volunteers, users, sponsors and other supporters. Because community currencies are founded on these people, it is crucial to keep this network up-to-date with developments.

Newsletters, regular blog updates, internal planning meetings and external canvassing events can facilitate such ongoing communication. Some ways to do this are:

- Linking up with local projects and businesses that participate in the currency to celebrate each other's milestones with online content or events.

- Celebrating success – keep up the morale of volunteer support workers by giving regular thanks and recognition for their services in bringing the currency to life.

- Speaking to users – testimonials from currency users provide great educational and marketing material. Capture these as blog entries to keep website content fresh.

Maintaining this level of activity requires substantial effort and resources and needs to be carefully considered in project planning and budgeting. Integrating a communications strategy into the project implementation and management plan ensures sufficient resources for effective communications at all stages of the project.

Communications are key to any project's success. However, it is not simply a case of generating as much coverage as possible, but rather of managing exposure to suit the project's needs, capacity and objectives. As such, communications must be tailored, focused and controlled – more is not always better. Any strategy, like all other aspects of a currency project, will benefit from rigorous evaluation. It is to this subject that the next and final chapter turns.

Chapter 08

EVALUATION – DEFINING AND MEASURING IMPACT

Measuring the impact of community currencies is challenging but essential to the further evolution and refinement of both individual projects and the field as a whole. This chapter provides advice and guiding principles that may be helpful when evaluating a currency's effectiveness.

For the currency design field as a whole, it is crucial to map the impact of the schemes currently in operation. For geographically and sectorally dispersed projects to learn from one another and professionalise the field, evidence of impact must be measured and shared. As each currency model evolves to better meet its objectives, new currencies emerge with hybrid models answering to new objectives. Because of this continuous process of development, getting a snapshot of successes and shortcomings is a big task.

Up to now, there has been a deficit of impact results coming from currency projects, resulting in certain landmark examples being regularly drawn upon as a proof of concept for others. This, however, is starting to change. With more interest and funding now coming from the public sector, currency projects are stepping up to the impact-assessment challenge.

Getting started

Evaluation is a crucial component of the design, implementation and running of any currency project that claims to have meaningful impact. Demonstrating success in achieving the project's aims is critical for securing funding and other types of support.

Currency initiatives often emerge from grand ambitions such as 'changing how money works' or 'strengthening the local economy'. Without translating these aspirations into clear short-term outcomes that can be measured, projects struggle to get an evaluation process off the ground. Ideally, evaluation should be integrated into the project from the outset; having a clear understanding of what the aims are helps to clarify the strategy to achieve them.

There is, however, no one way to evaluate a currency scheme. The choice between in-house evaluation, commissioning external expertise, or partnering with a university depends both on the resources available and the purpose of the evaluation.

A good starting point is to develop a theory of change (TOC), working backwards from the desired outcomes to understand how these can best be measured. TOC is a methodology for bringing about social change that starts from the desired outcomes, identifying all the stakeholders, processes, resources, and indicators to monitor and evaluate the progress towards the targeted outcomes. For a step-by-step guide for hosting a TOC workshop for a community currency project, see the guide No Small Change (in further reading).

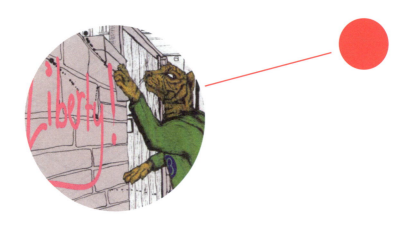

What to measure

Good impact evaluations measure what is important, not just what is easiest to count. This is likely to include a mix of social, economic and environmental outcomes and should ideally reflect what the currency users value. Once decided, desired outcomes can be broken down into clear and measurable indicators. For example, if the outcome is 'reducing social isolation in the local area', the number of people newly taking part in regular social activities since being involved with the currency might be a good indicator.

When mapping out a TOC, it is useful to organise these outcomes and indicators into short-, medium- and long-term goals, as seen in the flow diagram below produced for Spice Time-credit systems in South Wales.

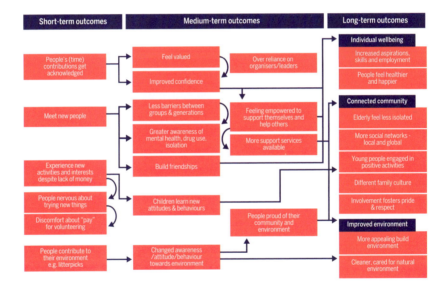

When to measure

It is advisable to gather baseline data before a project starts, or before a new participant joins the scheme with, for example, a brief new-user survey. This allows change to be captured at regular intervals and attributed more confidently to the currency project, rather than other developments in the locality or community.

A TOC can be used at almost any stage of development, from an initial idea to a long-established currency project – differing slightly depending on the project stage:

- **Looking backwards to evaluate:** Many people use a TOC as the basis of their evaluation strategy. For established projects, relatively more time may be spent trying to pull out indicators to measure progress towards the desired outcomes.

- **Looking forward to plan:** A TOC is useful for projects in the planning phase. Many groups may intend to start a project, but still have to decide what sort of currency they want to create. In this case, the focus may be more on understanding what the stakeholders want to achieve and the resources available to implement the project. This then determines the next steps to take.

Who to involve

Ensure that participants involved in evaluations are representative of the end-users of the project, rather than cherry-picking the best examples. If possible, compare evaluation outcomes from currency participants against a control group who have not taken part in the project. A good way to develop a TOC is to bring key stakeholders together in a workshop. This facilitates discussion and debate as to what the shared goals of the project are and how they can be achieved.

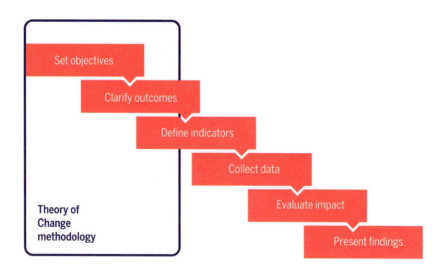

Theory of Change methodology

How to measure

There will be opportunities to collect data when the currency is up and running, such as through participants' online accounts. Data collection tools such as surveys, focus groups and project monitoring can also be used.

Choosing the right indicators

Once desired outcomes have been agreed, these can be broken down into measurable indicators. It is important to think carefully about what the right indicators are, as these are likely to be different in the short- and long-term. There may be a trade-off between things that are easier to measure and factors that most accurately reflect the project's goals: counting how many people use the currency scheme, for example, is much easier than determining whether this has had a positive impact on their lives.

Collecting data

Collecting both output and outcomes data is advisable. In the short-term, outputs can be valid indicators to inform some outcome measures. For example, the number of currency users and the quantity of transactions may be important in enabling the currency to achieve its objectives. There are several useful methods for collecting data:

User surveys

These indicate whether a currency meets user expectations, what people experience through its use and whether it noticeably impacted on their lives. Questions can be organised under themes: for example, the desirability or feasibility of the currency, satisfaction about the model, or changes in user behaviour since participating.

Questions can be qualitative – 'What do you think about the atmosphere in the neighbourhood?' – and/or quantitative – 'How often do you need assistance with using the currency?' A combination of both qualitative and quantitative questions provides the best insight, uncovering information about what people expect or have experienced, as well as why this might be the case. When devising a questionnaire it is advisable to compare and learn from other similar surveys.

Questionnaires asking about project outcomes after an event are not always convincing as they miss those who did not engage and cannot then analyse why this was so. Furthermore, people often want to give the answer they think the questioner wants to hear. It is better to measure how far users have come from where they were before the event.

This requires collecting outcomes data at consistent intervals over time, starting before any other activity. Even if measuring 'before and after' information, it will still be difficult to attribute any changes to the project. This is where it is useful to identify a comparison group who didn't take part in the project or didn't participate as much as other people.

Measuring impact of currency features

The Brixton Pound – what change does using the currency make?

When the Brixton Pound launched 'Payroll Local' – a project allowing council staff to take some salary in the currency – they compared outcomes between people who signed up to take part, against those who showed an interest in taking part.

Most changes were only experienced by the former group. For example, 40% of people taking B£s in their salary reported going out at lunchtime in Brixton more often, compared to less than 2% of those who didn't. More than 40% of even those who didn't sign up felt the project showed that Lambeth Council was innovative and 25% felt greater pride in the local area. These figures were even higher for those accepting B£ as part of their salary.

Focus groups

Focus groups can flesh out an evaluation with detailed responses from participants. These sessions are an opportunity to speak to specific user-groups about their feelings and probe more deeply into their experience of taking part in the project. They are also a useful tool for the project-planning stages, giving insight into the specifics of a problem or issue the currency aims to address, from the eyes of the target users.

Outputs data and accounting systems

Output data is best collected through electronic means. If a currency is counted solely through its material movements – for example, through the passing of paper notes – counting tends to be laborious and fairly inaccurate as notes can be lost or double counted.

Keeping an accounting record that includes hard output data on currency usage – such as which demographic is using the currency, how many times exchanges are made, what is the value of exchanges, how long are currency units generally in circulation before being converted back? – gives essential insight into the process, or the 'how', of the currency usage. This provides a framework from which more qualitative questions of 'why' the currency is functioning as it is can be asked.

Using embedded data collection

Since launching in 2012, the Hull and East Riding timebank has been collecting data from all new members through pre-test and post-test surveys. These surveys were co-designed in a workshop with nine timebank brokers from around the UK, helping to ensure that they captured change.

The timebank co-ordinator saw the benefits of collecting data and was willing to invest time in explaining to members why the research was important – thereby achieving a nearly 100% response rate from new members. The broker has also committed time to collecting data for follow-up surveys, with a current response rate of 35%. This will increase as the timebank develops further.

It is often tempting to push evaluation down the list of priorities, but assessment of a project's impact is a stage that should be integrated into any strategy. While it may seem overwhelming at first, ultimately envisioning a currency project in holistic terms from the outset is the surest way to success. We hope that this book and our corresponding evaluation guidebook *No Small Change* will help readers to do just this.

CONCLUSION — MORE CURRENCIES ARE BETTER THAN ONE

In regionally diverse and digitally advanced economies – whether local, national or sectoral – there is no one-size-fits-all money. What is more, though money evolves along with social and technological changes, it must not be forgotten that *people* ultimately control its path. In towns, regions and online networks people have quietly been creating their own currencies for decades: testament to the growing realisation that monetary innovation is not the exclusive purview of governments and big business.

Strong, active communities make for more resilient financial systems, while improving peoples' livelihoods and standards of living. Currencies can be designed to support this, to foster the kind of social interactions and exchanges we want, rather than remaining dependent on pounds, dollars and euros. This realisation is now moving decisively into the mainstream. As it becomes more and more clear that monetary monocultures serve the international financial markets better than the needs of people and societies, currency experiments are increasingly emerging as welcome disruptions to this *status quo*.

We hope that *People Powered Money* has addressed many of the questions arising from the growing community of community currency practitioners and supporters. By sharing the expertise of the partners in the CCIA project, and our many predecessors and colleagues, we hope our work will strengthen the ground from which future currencies can launch – prompting evermore responses to the challenge of how to make money work for people.

Endnotes / References

1 McCleay, M., Radia, A. and Thomas, R. (2014) Money Creation in the Modern Economy. Bank of England Quarterly, 2014 Q1. Download at: http://www.bankofengland.co.uk/publications/Documents/quarterlybulletin/2014/qb14q1prereleasemoneycreation.pdf

2 Ryan-Collins, J. & Greenham, T. (2012) *Where Does Money Come From?* London: New Economics Foundation. Pg 145-6

3 Blanc, J. (2011) Classifying 'CCs': Community, Complementary and Local Currencies, International Journal of Community Currency Research, Vol. 15 pp4-10.

4 Kennedy, M., Schuster, L., Martignoni, J. and Bindewald, L. (2013). *YES to a Parallel Currency approach for Greece!* Download at: http://www.monneta.org/index.php?id=165&kat=72

5 Varoufakis, Y. (2014) BITCOIN: *A flawed currency blueprint with a potentially useful application for the Eurozone.* Download at: http://yanisvaroufakis.eu/2014/02/15/bitcoin-a-flawed-currency-blueprint-with-a-potentially-useful-application-for-the-eurozone/

6 Slay, J. and Penny, J. (2014) *Commissioning for Outcomes and Co-production: a practical guide for local authorities.* London: New Economics Foundation. Download at: http://b.3cdn.net/nefoundation/974bfd0fd635a9ffcd_j2m6b04bs.pdf

7 Richards, M. (2014). *Bangla-Pesa Survey Results Feb 2014.* Koru Kenya. Available at: http://koru.or.ke/bangla-pesa-survey-feb-2014

8 Ward, B. and Lewis, J. (2002) Plugging the Leaks: *Making the most of every pound that enters your local economy.* London: New Economics Foundation. Download at http://www.neweconomics.org/publications/entry/plugging-the-leaks

9 Ferreirer, J. and Perry, M. (2015) *Spending Time with Money: From shared values to social connectivity.* CSCW '15 Proceedings of the 18th ACM Conference on Computer Supported Cooperative Work & Social Computing pg 1222-1234

10 Steed, S. (2013) *Money and Giving: do financial incentives deter or encourage co-operative behaviour?* Pg 19. London: New Economics Foundation. Download at: http://b.3cdn.net/nefoundation/2927a207e52f267882_80m6iy5zu.pdf; Bindewald, L. and Steed, S. (2014) *No Small Change: Evaluating the success of your community currency project.* Pg 45-6 London: New Economics Foundation. Download at http://b.3cdn.net/nefoundation/6e006679e8a6d649fd_3num6frei.pdf

11 Apteligen Consultants (2014) *An Evaluation of Spice Time Credits.* Download at: http://www.justaddspice.org/app/uploads/2015/01/Spice-Evaluation_Apteligen-Report-MAIN-REPORT1.pdf

12 Ryan-Collins, J., Greenham, T., Bindewald, L. and Schuster, L. (2013) *Energising Money: An introduction to energy currencies and accounting.* London: New Economics Foundation. Download at: http://b.3cdn.net/nefoundation/d5efb739f3fb9a137c_q2m6y7916.pdf

13 Slay, J. and Penny, J. (2014) *Commissioning for Outcomes and Co-production: A practical guide for local authorities.* London: New Economics Foundation. Download at: http://b.3cdn.net/nefoundation/974bfd0fd635a9ffcd_j2m6b04bs.pdf; Stephens, L. and Ryan-Collins, J. (2008) *Co-production: A manifesto for growing the core economy.* London: New Economics Foundation. Download at: http://www.neweconomics.org/publications/entry/co-production

14 Bindewald, L. and Steed, S. (2014) *No Small Change: Evaluating the success of your community currency project.* Pg 25-37. Download at: http://b.3cdn.net/nefoundation/6e006679e8a6d649fd_3num6frei.pdf

15 Ryan-Collins, J. & Greenham, T. (2012) *Where Does Money Come From?* London: New Economics Foundation. Chapter 3.

16 CCIA has produced several more detailed documents on the matter including a checklist for practitioners, visit http://community-currency.info/en/find/cc-toolkits/legal-and-compliance/

17 Ryan-Collins, J. & Greenham, T. (2012) *Where Does Money Come From?* London: New Economics Foundation. Pg 7.

18 'Software for community currencies' (2015). Access at: http://community-currency.info/en/glossary/software-for-community-currencies/

FURTHER RESOURCES

Online knowledge gateway

http://community-currency.info

A gateway to online resources, literature and general knowledge on community and complementary currencies. It was published by CCIA in 2014 and is maintained by international partners and volunteer contributors.

Visit the site for:

- Quick introductions to the field for policy makers, researchers and SMEs

- Evaluation guidebook 'No Small Change: Evaluating the success of your currency project'

- Published results from CCIA and beyond: 'Money with a purpose: Community currencies achieving social, environmental and economic impact'

- Guidance on legal and compliance issues

- Details of community currencies in operation across the world

Journals

International Journal of Community Currency Research (IJCCR):
http://ijccr.net/

The IJCCR is a peer-reviewed, online journal that provides free access to the latest knowledge and research on community currencies. It aims to provide a common forum for informed debate on the empirical, critical and theoretical research and to bridge the communication gap between currency activists and academics.

Further reading

Practical community currency guides

Community Currency Guide (2006), by Bernard Lietaer and Gwendolyn Hallsmith. Global Community Initiatives. Download at: http://www.lietaer.com/2009/12/community-currency-guide/

Guide pratique de monnaies complémentaires (2013), by Antoine Attout, Léone Clerc, Amandine Cloot, Antoine Fain, Lise Disneur, Arnaud Marchand and Laurence Roland. Download at: https://www.financite.be/fr/article/guide-pratique-des-monnaies-complementaires

'Legal and Compliance overview' on Community-Currency.info. Access at: http://community-currency.info/en/find/cc-toolkits/legal-and-compliance/

Local Money: how to make it happen in your community (2010), by Peter North. Totnes, United Kingdom: Transition Books.

Maak je buurt uitmuntend! (2014), by Bernard Lietaer, Anne Snick and Edgar Kampers, published by the Flemish government. Download at: http://www.vlaanderen.be/nl/publicaties/detail/maak-je-buurt-uitmuntend-handboek-gemeenschapsmunten-voor-lokale-besturen-en-organisaties

'Money with a purpose' (2015), by Susan Steed and Leander Bindewald. London, United Kingdom: New Economics Foundation. Download at: http://www.neweconomics.org/publications/entry/money-with-a-purpose

No Small Change: Evaluating the success of your community currency project (2013), by Leander Bindewald and Susan Steed. London, United Kingdom: New Economics Foundation. Download at http://community-currency.info/en/find/cc-toolkits/evaluation/

People Money: the promise of regional currencies (2012), by Margrit Kennedy, Bernard Lietaer and John Rogers. Axminster, United Kingdom: Triarchy Press. http://valueforpeople.co.uk/peoplemoney

Community/complementary currency theory

'Classifying 'CCs': Community, Complementary and Local Currencies' (2011), by Jérôme Blanc. International Journal of Community Currency Research, Vol. 15.

Creating Wealth: growing local economies with local currencies (2011), by Gwendolyn Hallsmith and Bernard Lietaer. Gabriola Island, Canada: New Society Publishers.

Currencies of transition: transforming money to unleash sustainability (2013), by Jem Bendell and Thomas H Greco. In Malcolm McIntosh, (ed) *The Necessary Transition: the journey towards the sustainable enterprise economy*. Sheffield, United Kingdom: Greenleaf Publishing Limited.

Residual Barter Systems and Macro-economic Stability: Switzerland's Wirtschaftsring (2007), by James Stodder. Download at: http://www.lietaer.com/images/Stodder_WIR_paper2009.pdf

Economics and theories of money

The End of Money and the Future of Civilization (2009), by Thomas H. Greco. Vermont, United States: Chelsea Green Publishing.

The Future of Money: creating new wealth, work and a wiser world (2001), by Bernard Lietaer. London, United Kingdom: Random House

Money and Giving: do financial incentives deter or encourage co-operative behaviour? (2013), by Susan Steed. London, United Kingdom: New Economics Foundation. Download at: http://www.neweconomics.org/publications/entry/money-and-giving

Money and Sustainability: the missing link (2012), by Bernard Lietaer, Christian Arnsperger, Sally Goerner and Stefan Brunnhuber. Axminster, United Kingdom: Triarchy Press

Money Creation in the Modern Economy (2014), by Michael McCleay, Amer Radia and Ryland Thomas. Bank of England Quarterly, 2014, Q1. Download at: http://www.bankofengland.co.uk/publications/Documents/quarterlybulletin/2014/qb14q1prereleasemoneycreation.pdf

Occupy Money: creating an economy where everybody wins (2012), by Margrit Kenndy. Gabriola Island, Canada: New Society Publishers

The Heretic's Guide to Global Finance: Hacking the Future of Money (2013), by Brett Scott. London: Pluto Press.

The Social Life of Money (2014), by Nigel Dodd. Princeton, United States: Princeton University Press.

Where Does Money Come From? (2012), by Josh Ryan-Collins and Tony Greenham. London, United Kingdom: New Economics Foundation.

Other

Commissioning for Outcomes and Co-production: a practical guide for local authorities (2014), by Julia Slay and Joe Penny. London: New Economics Foundation. Download at: http://b.3cdn.net/nefoundation/974bfd0fd635a9ffcd_j2m6b04bs.pdf

Co-production: a manifesto for growing the core economy (2008), by Lucie Stephens and Josh Ryan-Collins. London, United Kingdom: New Economics Foundation. Download at: http://www.neweconomics.org/publications/entry/co-production

Plugging the Leaks: making the most of every pound that enters your local economy (2002) Bernie Ward and Julie Lewis. London, United Kingdom: New Economics Foundation. Download at http://www.neweconomics.org/publications/entry/plugging-the-leaks

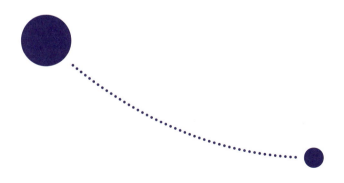

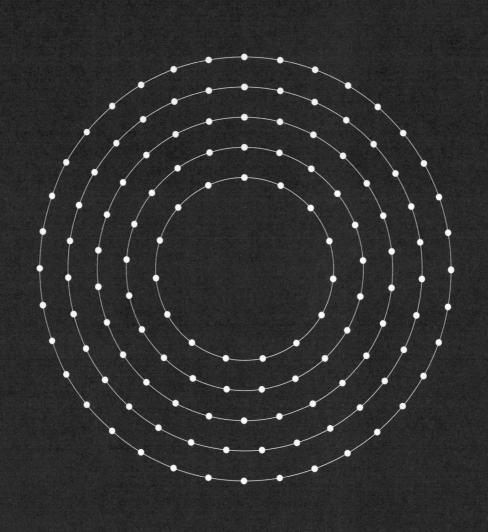

GLOSSARY

Glossary

Backing: a design feature of currency (conventional or otherwise), which – in the broader sense – guarantees the long-term purchasing power of a currency. In the narrower, the issuer guarantees to exchange the currency for either another currency or a commodity.

Bonus: in the community currency field, 'bonus' refers to a premium paid to individuals and organisations directly exchanging a conventional currency for a community currency. For example, £100 of the former 'buys' £110 of the latter at the point of exchange – even though these remain pegged one-to-one for purposes of all other transactions. This effectively gives users a 10% discount when making purchases in the community currency, incentivising its use.

Business-to-business trade exchange: currency systems operating in a network of businesses to which consumer households typically do not have access. The term is often used synonymously with business barter systems, reciprocal exchange systems, capacity trade systems. These currencies typically operate by the mutual-credit methodology, with exceptions like the WIR bank in Switzerland. Many such currencies are operated by commercial companies.

Clearing system: this serves as an intermediary accounting system between members of a network, settling accounts often and grouping transactions at regular intervals – for example, at the end of each business day – and calculating each member's new balance.

Closed-loop payment systems: refers to a) a strictly limited network of users (usually through membership), outside of which the currency cannot be spent and b) a design feature of the currency itself, which cannot be exchanged for national currency. Closed-loop payment systems aim to keep wealth within a defined community of users and increase the volume and frequency of exchanges between those users. The most famous example of this type of system is the Swiss WIR Bank, as well as many other business-to-business trade exchanges.

Collateral: refers to any asset – typically capital or property, but also financial assets – used to guarantee settlement of debt in the case of default.

Community currencies: a subset of complementary currencies that are tied to a specific, demarcated and limited community. This community could be, for example, geographical (local currencies); business-based (mutual-credit systems); or online (global digital currencies). As such, a community currency is designed to meet the needs of this defined community, typically on a not-for-profit basis.

Complementary currencies: currencies designed to sit alongside mainstream money to address objectives that the conventional money system can't.

Convertible currency: a currency that can be converted into another currency. For example, Brixton Pounds can be exchanged one-to-one for pounds sterling; while the WIR franc is – theoretically at least – not convertible and there are penalties for attempting to convert it into Swiss francs.

Co-production: goes beyond mere consultation or participation of the users of a service to promote their active involvement in all stages of that service's design and delivery. Regarding community currencies, co-production can be effective in ensuring that the design of the project aligns with the needs of users.

Core economy: the social 'operating system' on which the 'software' of the mainstream market economy depends. It includes any productive work – such as child-rearing or informal care – which is necessary for the functioning of the formal economy, but which is not given a value in monetary terms by that economy.

Countercyclical: refers to any economic policy, effect or phenomenon inversely related to fluctuations in the economy overall – that is, when the economy expands, the countercyclical element shrinks and vice-versa. Community currencies frequently have this quality, which allows them to match supply and demand in the context of contraction in the conventional money supply.

Crowdfunding: the practice of funding a project or venture by raising many small amounts of money from a large number of people or organisations, typically via the internet. This contrasts with previous fundraising models that tended to raise a large amount of money from a few people or organisations.

Demurrage: a system of 'negative interest', whereby the value of a currency decreases over time. In the community currency field, demurrage is typically used to encourage spending and discourage hoarding. The German monetary and social reformer Silvio Gesell was the first to propose built-in depreciation of a currency in his Freigeldtheorie, which contrasted money's retention of value with the depreciation of natural goods. If the monetary system had a negative interest rate or some other form of demurrage, people would buy goods more readily and would invest their time and effort in the maintenance of their stock.

Denomination: A 'denomination' refers to a specific 'amount' of a given currency, which is represented through a physical or electronic medium of exchange, determining the quantities in which a given currency can actually be obtained. For example, pound sterling (currency) is issued in coins and notes (media of exchange) which have specific values (denominations). Denomination thus differs from the unit of account.

E-money Directive: an EU directive determining legislation around the regulation of electronic forms of legal tender money. The implementation in the different member states varies. The E-money Directive also aims to increase competition and participation in this industry by opening it up to non-banks.

Freigeldtheorie: developed by German economist Silvio Gesell, Freigeldtheorie (free money theory) contrasted money's ability to retain value with the tendency of all other commodities to devalue over time. See demurrage.

Futures: a contract obliging a buyer to purchase an asset – typically a commodity or financial instrument – at a set price at a specified time in the future. Intended to protect sellers from volatile market fluctuations, 'futures' are regularly cited as a source of economic instability, as they encourage market speculation by investors who gamble on commodity prices.

Hoarding: the act of accumulating a large quantity of capital without any intention of re-investing it back into the economy.

Inflation: The rate at which the general level of prices for goods and services is rising, and, subsequently, purchasing power is falling.

Issuance: the act of putting new money into circulation, typically through state spending or – much more commonly these days – the extension of credit/creation of debt by private financial institutions.

Leakage / leaky bucket theory: the hypothesis that more money 'leaks' out of a community than is put in. This occurs because profits accrue to corporations, which increasingly are registered outside of the locality, meaning that the wealth created through a community's economic activity is ultimately reinvested or hoarded elsewhere.

Legal tender: a means of payment that is recognised and guaranteed by law and must be accepted by any state, organisation or individual in settlement of debt. Legal tender money is most readily accepted as a means of paying taxes; and legal tender savings with licensed, deposit-taking institutions (banks) are guaranteed by many states up to certain amount.

Legal tender-backed currency: refers to a complementary currency with guaranteed redeemability (backing) for the legal tender of the country in which it operates. The Brixton Pound, for example, falls into this category, as it is redeemable by businesses for pound sterling.

LETS: Local Exchange Trading Schemes. Members trade skills, services and resources with each other, using credits issued by members themselves at the moment of exchange. LETS thereby mobilise a community's latent capacity by providing both a forum and medium of exchange outside the conventional market economy. Typically LETS operate by the mutual-credit methodology.

Liquidity: refers to the extent to which a commodity or asset can be bought or sold without its value being affected. Liquidity also denotes the ease with which any given asset can be transformed into cash through sale.

Local authority: a branch of government responsible for local administration. The precise remit of local authorities varies from country to country and even within countries.

Malus: within the community currency field, a 'malus' is the opposite of a 'bonus', disincentivising the exchange of a community currency for national currency. An individual or organisation wanting to redeem their community currency for its national equivalent would receive, for example, only £90 of the latter in exchange for £100 of the former: with both currencies having the same purchasing power within all other transactions, this effectively imposes a 10% penalty.

Medium of exchange: the actual medium used to conduct financial transactions, whether physical (notes and coins) or electronic (data representing account balances, transferred via credit or debit cards or online systems).

Mutual credit: a system by which units of credit are created at the moment of the transaction between individual users as a debit of one's account and a credit of the other's. Operating within agreed limits of credit and debt, members of a mutual-credit system effectively loan one another the capital necessary for the exchange of goods and services within the network, with the overall balance of all members' accounts always equalling zero.

Non-convertible pegged currency: A currency that is not directly convertible into legal tender, but is pegged at par with the national currency.

One-planet living: a bioregional and WWF-led campaign for a more equal and sustainable use of the planet's resources, using ecological and carbon footprinting as its main indicators.

Par / pegged at par: of equal value. If a community or complementary currency is pegged at par with pound sterling, for example, it means that one unit of the currency is worth one pound.

Payment Services Directive: an EU directive aiming to regulate payment services and payment service providers throughout the European Union and European Economic Area. The Payment Services Directive also aims to increase competition and participation in this industry by opening it up to non-banks.

Pro-sumer: a term used in contrast with the more familiar 'consumer' to indicate that nobody only ever consumes but also produces in some capacity and thus has an active role within the shaping of the economy.

Redeemability: the ability to/act of exchanging a currency or voucher for a good, service or other currency. In the broader sense this could be with any other user of the respective currency, in the narrower sense this only describes guarantees by the issuer of the currency (backing).

Reward currencies: incentivise certain behaviour by consumers, such as the purchase of more sustainable products, through earning points that can be redeemed for rewards or discounts on future purchases.

SME: an initialisation of Small and Medium-sized Enterprise. The SME economy is often contrasted with the economic domination of national and multinational corporations and is a key part of many environmentalist economic approaches. According to European standards, an SME is defined as a business with 250 employees or fewer and an annual turnover not exceeding €50 million and/or annual balance sheet not exceeding €43 million.

Store of value: the characteristic of retaining value or – in the case of currencies – purchasing power over a long period of time.

Theory of change (TOC): a methodology for bringing about social change that starts from the desired outcomes, identifying all the stakeholders, processes, resources, and indicators to monitor and evaluate the progress towards the targeted outcomes.

Timebank: a network through which members offer and request services and skills to and from one another, with transactions following the principle that one hour's work equals one unit (often denominated in hours). A broker might help to match offers and needs in the community. Typically timebanks operate by the mutual-credit methodology.

Time currency / time-credits: apart from timebanks in the narrower use of the word, other currencies are denominated and valued in units of time without operating by the mutual-credit methodology.

Transition currencies: UK-based community currencies affiliated with the Transition Town movement, which aim to further that movement's goals of rebuilding self-sufficient local economies that are environmentally sustainable and socially oriented. These have included: the Bristol, Brixton, Totnes, Stroud and Lewes Pounds. While each has unique features, all are valued one-to-one with pound sterling for transaction purposes and all fall under the basic legal backed tender currency type.

Transition Town: a global network of local groups seeking to move towards a more sustainable, socially-oriented and local/community-driven economy. Community currencies are often part of this wider project, as with the 'transition pounds' in the UK.

Unit of account: the standard unit of measurement allowing common evaluation of value and cost. Along with being a 'store of value' and 'medium of exchange', acting as a unit of account is one of the key core functions of conventional money.

Wellbeing: a concept that refers to the physical, psychological, social, medical and economic state of an individual or group. According to advocates of wellbeing, indicators of how people experience their lives should be at the centre of government policy, rather than a crude measurement of economic growth.

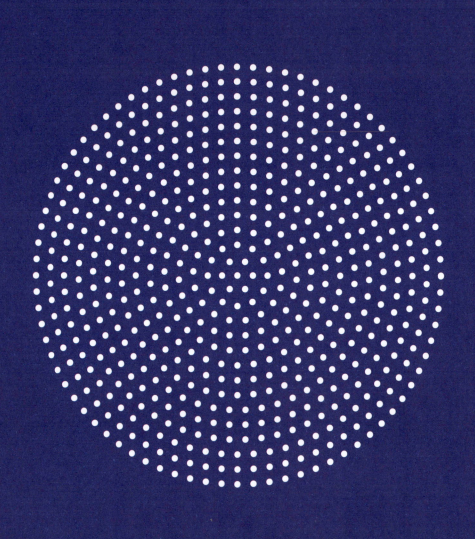

INDEX

Index

A
accountability 119
accounting systems/practices 114, 155
advertising, selling 124
anti-counterfeit measures 114
apps, use of 57, 103
Argentina (Trueque) 37–8
audiences, target 137–40
Austria (Wörgl) 34

B
backers 70
backing 108–9, 171
Banco Palmas 51–2
Bangla-Pesa 50
banks, community 51–2
barter networks 37–8
Beki 124, 125
Belgium
   e-Portemonnee 64, 74–5, 82–3, 103, 107, 109
  Eco-Iris 66
  RES 124, 125
  Terra 65
  Torekes 40
benefit payments 127
BerkShares 51
Bitcoin
  convertibility of 112
  denomination and transaction media 103
  description of 102
  issuance 106
Bolo, Pascal 53
bonus (and malus) 111, 171
Brazil (Palmas) 51–2
Bristol City Council 40, 78
Bristol Pound
  and City Council 40, 78
  and council tax payments 78
  and financial regulations 129
  and Mayor's wages 79
  social effects of 56–7
Brixton Pound
  backing methods 109
  bonus and malus 111, 124
  convertibility of 112
  denomination and transaction media 57, 103
  description of 56
  evaluation of impact 57, 154
  fees 124
  financing mechanisms 124, 125
  issuance 105, 107
  and local council 40
  and merchandise, selling 125
  payment options 57, 101, 134–5
  social effects of 56, 57, 154
  wages in currency 57, 154
budgeting 120–1
business networks 50–1
business plan 120–1
business-to-business systems 35, 50, 171

C
Cahn, Edgar 36
canvassing 144
care services, provision of 40, 47, 60–1
cash flow, improving 49–50
CES (Community Exchange System) 133
championing (stakeholders) 79
Chiemgauer
  demurrage 124

description of 54
leakage 125
circulation, into and out of 106–7
clearing system 171
closed-loop systems 40, 113, 125, 126, 171
co-partnering 74, 77
co-production 46, 47–8, 71, 80–1, 172
communications strategy
   clear message 141–5
   and currency appearance 141
   infographics 142
   key messages of 138–40
   logo 141
   maintaining a network 146
   media, use of 143, 145
   meetings and events 144
   online communications 142–3
   press and public affairs 145
   printed material 141
   social media 143
   target audiences 137–40
   websites 142–3
community banks 51–2
community cohesion 55–8
community currency concept
   definition 32, 172
   historical background 31–6
community currency features
   convertibility of 112–13, 172
   demurrage 32, 34, 39, 54, 100, 110, 118, 124, 173
   denomination 101, 103
   function of the currency 99–100
   issuance 104–7, 174
   market creation 114–15
   network membership 114–15
   security measures 113–14
   transaction media 101–3

community currency objectives
   cash flow, improving 49–50
   core economy, supporting 61
   democratising services and organisations 44–8
   education of consumers 55–6
   leakage prevention 52–5
   meeting community needs 45–8
   network creation 50–1
   new ways to transact 57
   social effects 45–8, 55–7, 58–61
   social participation 58–61
   spare capacity, using 52
   supporting SME economy 49–58
Community Exchange System (CES) 133
complementary currencies 31–3, 172
conceptualisation process 93
conferences 144
continuation stage 95
convertible currencies 112–13, 172
core economy 61, 172
corporation tax 127
costs of implementation 120–1
council tax payment 78
councillors 145
countercyclical effects 34, 172
counterfeiting, prevention of 114
Creditos 37–8
crowdfunding 172
currency, paper-based 29–30
customer loyalty 55–7

D

data collection (for evaluation) 153–5
data protection 129
decision-making 78, 119
democratising services and organisations 44–8

demurrage
  and Chiemgauer 54
  concept of 100, 110, 124, 173
  pros and cons 110, 118, 124
  Regiogeld 39
  scrip money 32
  Wörgl 34
denomination 101, 103, 173
design of currency 141
design process of currency 89–95
digital currencies *see* Bitcoin; CES; e-Portemonnee; RES; SolarCoin; SoNantes; TradeQoin; Ven; WIR Bank

E
E-money Directive (EU) 128, 173
e-Portemonnee
  backing methods 109
  denomination and transaction media 103
  description of 64, 82–3
  impact of 82–3
  issuance 107
  and stakeholder integration 74–5
Eco-Iris 66
education of consumers 55–6
EKO 55
elderly care 36, 40, 47, 60–1
Ely Time Credits 62
empowerment 48, 62
energy currencies 64–5, 82–3
engagement levels 71–9
environmental sustainability 38, 39, 55, 63–6
EU legislation 128, 173, 175
Eusko 54
evaluation of impact
  how to measure 153–5
  importance of 150
  of pilot stage 94
  and theory of change 150–2, 176
  what to measure 151
  when to measure 151–2
exchange fees 124
exploration (planning phase) 92

F
feasibility study 93
features of currency *see* community currency features
fees 124
financial regulations 128–30
financing the scheme 120–5
Findhorn 55
focus groups 154
France
  Eusko 54
  and financial regulations 128
  SoNantes 40, 53, 103, 107, 109, 142
fraud, prevention of 114
Freigeldtheorie 173
function of the currency 99–100
fundraising 120–5
futures 173

G
Germany
  Chiemgauer 54, 124, 125
  and financial regulations 128
  Regiogeld 39, 54
Ghent 40
governance 118–19
Great Depression 33–4

H
health benefits 63
hoarding 54, 100, 110, 173
Hull and East Riding Timebank 155

I

ICT 130–3, 142–3
impact evaluation *see* evaluation of impact
implementation and operation of currency
   budgeting 120–1
   business plan 120–1
   costs 121
   financial issues 120–5, 128–30
   fundraising 123–5
   insurance 129
   legal framework 126–30
   non-linear process 90–2
   organisational structure and governance 118–19
   piloting phase 93–4
   planning phase 92–3
   taxation 126–7
income tax 127
incorporation, types of 119
inequality, countering 58–62, 63, 72
inflation 65, 106–7, 174
infographics 142
insurance 129
integration (stakeholder) 72, 74–5
issuance 104–7, 174

K

Kenya (Bangla-Pesa) 50
Kruggerand 103–4

L

Lambeth Council 16, 40, 57, 154
leading (stakeholder) 72
leakage 52–5, 125, 174
legal framework 126–30
legal tender-backed currency 126, 127, 174

LETS (Local Exchange Trading Systems)
   description of 35–6, 174
   and quantity of money 105
   and taxation 126
Lietaer, Bernard 65
Limburg *see* e-Portemonnee
Linton, Michael 35
liquidity 174
local authority involvement 39–40, 45, 47, 56–7, 72–3, 77, 78, 145
local councillors 145
Local Exchange Trading Systems (LETS) *see* LETS
logo 141
London *see* Brixton Pound
loyalty cards/schemes 48, 56, 103, 104, 109
loyalty, customer 55–7
Luxembourg (Beki) 124, 125

M

Makkie
   backing methods 109
   denomination and transaction media 103
   description of 48
   issuance 107
   and social participation 60–1, 72–3
   stakeholders 71–3
malus (and bonus) 111, 175
market analysis 92
market creation 114–15
media, use of 79, 138, 140, 143–5
medium of exchange 100, 175
meetings and events 144
membership fees 124
membership policy 114–15
merchandise, selling 125

Minsky, Hyman 114
multi-stakeholder challenges 79–80
mutual-credit systems 175
   see also Bangla-Pesa; CES; Hull and East Riding Timebank; LETS; SoNantes; TradeQoin

N
Nantes *see* SoNantes
Netherlands
   Makkie 48, 60–1, 71–3, 103, 107, 109
   and taxation 127
   TradeQoin 50, 52, 103, 107, 109, 124
networks
   creation of 50–1
   maintenance of 146
   membership of 114–15
newspapers 145
non-convertible pegged currency 127, 175

O
objectives of currency *see* community currency objectives
online communications 142–3
organisational structure and governance 118–19
outcomes, measuring *see* evaluation of impact
output data 155

P
Palmas 51–2
par/pegged at par 34, 175
participating (stakeholders) 78
partners (stakeholders) 70
pay-by-text 57, 134–5
Payment Services Directive (EU) 128, 175

piloting phase 93–5
planning phase 92–5
podcasts 143
policymakers 138, 140
politicians 145
press coverage 145
printed communications 141
pro-sumers 71, 175
public, communicating with 138, 145
public funding cuts 45, 47, 48
public sector role 39, 45, 47–8, 59, 73, 77, 129–30
publicity *see* communications strategy
purchased and redeemable vouchers 108

Q
QoinWare 130
quantity of money 105–6, 107
questionnaires, evaluation 153–4

R
redeemability 108, 109, 125, 176
Redes de Trueque 37–8
Regiogeld 39, 54
RES 124, 125
reward currency scheme 52, 64, 66, 176
risk perception 79

S
salary in currency 72, 79, 57, 154, 127
scaling-up 95
Scotland (EKO) 55
scrip money 31–2
security measures 113–14
self-worth 62
SME economy 34–5, 49–57, 176
social benefits 36, 55, 56–63, 73

social media 143
social security benefits 127
software 130, 132–3
solar power 65, 82
SolarCoin 65
SoNantes
   backing methods 109
   denomination and transaction media 103
   description of 40
   infographics 142
   issuance 107
   and local circulation of 53
South Africa
   CES 133
   Kruggerand 103–4
spare capacity, using 52
Spice Time Credits
   backing methods 109
   communications strategy 144
   and co-partnering 76–7
   denomination and transaction media 103
   description of 59, 60
   evaluation of impact 63, 96–7, 120, 151
   funding of 120
   health benefits of 63
   issuance 105, 107
   and outcome 151
   social benefits of 62, 96–7
   website 143
spokespeople, attracting 145
sponsorship 76
stakeholders
   and co-production 80–1
   and communications strategy 141–2
   and evaluation process 152
   groups of 70–1
   levels of engagement 71–9
   multi-stakeholder challenges 79–80
   and organisational structure 118–19
   and piloting phase 94
   and planning phase 93
stamp scrip 31–2
St.Gallen 40, 47
store of value 100, 176
surveys, users 151, 153–4, 155
sustainability 38, 39, 55, 63–6
Switzerland
   WIR Bank 34–5, 109, 112
   Zeitvorsoge 40, 47

T
tap and pay technology 57
taxation 126–7
Terra
   backing methods 109
   denomination and transaction media 103
   description of 65
text, payment by 57, 134–5
theory of change (TOC) 150–2, 176
time-credit/currency systems 36–7, 61, 176
   see also Makkie; Spice Time Credits; timebanks; Zeitvorsoge
timebanks
   backing methods 109
   and data collection 155
   description of 36–7, 176
   issuance 105
   and legal compliance 126, 127
   see also time-credit/currency systems
TOC (theory of change) 150–2, 176
Torekes 40
TradeQoin

backing methods 109
benefits of 52
denomination and transaction media 103
description of 50
fees 124
issuance 107
transaction fees 124
transaction media 101–3
transition currencies 176
transition towns 176, 177
transparency 119
Trueque 37–8

U
UK *see* Bristol Pound; Brixton Pound; EKO; Hull and East Riding Timebank; Spice Time Credits
unit of account 64–5, 99–100, 101, 103, 177
USA (BerkShares) 51
users
  communicating with 137–8, 141–6
  focus groups 154
  as stakeholders 71
  surveying 151, 153–4, 155

V
VAT 126–7
Ven 103
videos 143

W
wages in currency 72, 79, 57, 154, 127
websites 103, 130, 131, 141, 142–3
wellbeing 63, 177
WIR Bank
  backing method 109
  convertibility of 112

description of 34–5
Wörgl 34
workshops 144

Z
Zeitvorsoge 40, 47

Notes

Notes